Desmond Hogan was born in County Galway and now lives in London. In 1971 he won the Hennessy Award and in 1977 the Rooney prize. The Abbey Theatre produced two of his plays *A Short Walk to the Sea* and *Sanctified Distances* and BBC Radio 3 broadcast *Jimmy* in 1978. His first novel *The Ikon-Maker* was published initially in Ireland in 1976; when republished three years later in Great Britain it was a New Fiction Society choice. His collection of stories *The Diamonds at the Bottom of the Sea* was received with unusual acclaim. His work is also published in the United States.

D1125216

Desmond Hogan

The Leaves on Grey

PICADOR

published by Pan Books

First published 1980 by Hamish Hamilton Ltd
This Picador edition published 1981 by Pan Books Ltd,
Cavaye Place, London SW10 9PG
© Desmond Hogan 1980
ISBN 0 330 26287 4
Reproduced, printed and bound in Great Britain by
Cox & Wyman Ltd, Reading

for those who
made me welcome
in London

The abyss has swallowed my loved ones,
and my parents' home has been pillaged.

Marina Tsvetayeva

Acknowledgements I should like to thank Daniel J. Rooney of Pittsburg, and the Arts Council of the Irish Republic who encouraged me towards the passage of this novel. I am grateful to Martin Brian & O'Keeffe for permission to quote from two poems by Patrick Kavanagh.

Book One

THIS IS A STRANGE STORY. As I've just returned from seeing Liam I must go back to the beginning to tell where I think it all started, to try to shape events in a way you might understand.

When I speak of Liam I am speaking of a boy, beautiful, of a young man beloved by the women of Dublin, of a middle-aged man with a triad of expressions, adolescent, sage, nomad.

To seek the beginning is to go back a long time ago, when the town in which I am writing was a little different and trees hung at the end of the town, trees hung obsessively, many trees, much green at the end of the street come summer, come the arrival of leaves and sun and buttercup blaze.

I lived up the street from Liam, in a house equally big and composed of limestone. Next door was a cinema. Hedy Lamarr or Rita Hayworth prostrating themselves unduly there in the mornings when I was very small and made my first tentative strides up the street towards Liam's house.

He had a flock of rabbits, a flock of geese, dogs, cats, a rainbow of birds and animals. He led them like a young Francis of Assisi across a big green lawn, chiding them, reading them poetry. Sometimes even birds or animals died and when the war was waging in the outside world we buried them, he and I, a boy in a white sleeveless jersey, and me, a chubby child in a blue coat. There was one great oak in that garden, over the patch of earth in which peas grew, and there animals and birds were consigned. As he grew older Liam wore cloaks for this procedure, a druid against the grey skies.

Nearby was an orphanage. We were the privileged children of town, the extremely privileged, and we encountered the orphans sadly. They had nothing that we had: the food, the clothes, the homes, the parents; but they possessed the convent ground, marsh and grey sky and river always rushing, always tempting, a wild river that took the lives of farmers or farmers' wives who wandered with rosary beads in the hinterland of the town into the river.

Let me speak of the town, a grand old town built by an English landlord and possessed of fine streets and a mindfulness of the empire. In the men's club at the very end of our street, a little black hut, there were photographs of earnest young soldiers with riveting eyes and high cheekbones. This town sacrificed many of its working-class men to the Great War and, verging on adolescence, I recall reading Thomas Kettle – 'If I live I intend to spend the rest of my life working for perpetual peace. I have seen war and faced artillery and know what an outrage it is against simple men.'

Thomas Kettle was a young Irish poet killed in the First World War, a distant relative of Dr Kenneally, Liam's father. I found the quotation in a book in Liam's house and it changed life for me, I realized that day there was right and wrong, good and bad, that the world was subdivided into levels of opinion and in realizing this I began to notice Mrs Kenneally.

Mrs Kenneally was the Russian wife of Dr Kenneally; a lady beautiful, near middle age, with hair of gold. She had a firm body, a most statuesque figure and there at the end of the street standing, standing against the leaves, she was to one and all the most attractive person in town, something fallen from heaven, her chiffon scarf blurting out against the trees.

There was a maid in the house who was from Cork and she in her little kitchen hoarded herbs, hoarded parsley and paprika, and baked huge currant cakes or loaves of brown bread. While lounging in the garden on summer days Dr and Mrs Kenneally were served home-made orange juice by her. They'd have light refreshments instead of the wine they consumed in bucketfuls, drinking and celebrating and having parties.

More than anything the Kenneallys' was a house of parties. There beside the convent they entertained actors, writers, artists, famous surgeons and little known nuns. Always nuns seemed to sneak into the picture, nuns from the nearby convent or nuns from far away; nuns like spectators, keeping check.

4

As I grew older I touched upon these parties, touched upon the sight of them. They were held in the drawing-room. Earlier in childhood Liam built paper castles there for hamsters. Now music played, wine flowed, rosé wine, and a large painting over the fireplace, scarlet and black and skull white, edified an Aran woman. To these parties came the cream of the Irish artistic set, travelling in old cars like hearses or more elegant and recent vehicles. Once an artist journeyed from Dublin, the midland breezes whipping her hair.

Art, literature, politics were discussed.

Once an actor from a Shakespearian travelling company, at the time resident in the fair green, arrived in his Othello costume, complete with polish on his face, got drunk, then went into *De Profundis* by Oscar Wilde, standing on the table, taking off some of his clothes, not all of them. Eventually he was led away crying.

A frequent visitor was a famous Irish soprano who charmed visitors with songs like 'I have seen the lark in the morning', or 'Down by the Sally Gardens'.

The turf seemed to come specially from Connemara, roaring and spitting.

In autumn 1948 Liam and I started going to secondary school in the east of Ireland. At Christmas both of us, young males now, stood at a party while an old man from Connemara told ghost stories, the fire blazing, and a woman imperceptibly stood by, a woman dressed in black, a stained glass maker from Dublin come to design a window for the local church.

The whole cast of a recent production of *The White-headed Boy* by Lennox Robinson were there, a cleric over from Rome, the lead singer in the local operettas who sang 'Golden Days in Heidelberg'. Mrs Kenneally got quite drunk, drunk in a nice way, speaking Russian, saying a prayer in Russian, as doctors, actors, politicians murmured.

There was a new coalition government in power in Ireland that year and a secretary to the more radical of these parties was present, standing in the background.

5

Liam left the party when his mother got drunk. I later found him in an upstairs room, thumbing through beautifully illustrated books of Irish and Russian fairy-stories.

Back at school Liam kept saying, 'My mother is upset. My mother is upset.'

The school we were attending was situated near Dublin, nearer to the Curragh of Kildare, blackened now by winter it was where the young of the *haute bourgeoisie* of Ireland were sent, the sons of doctors and lawyers, namely the class to which Liam and I belonged. As rain beat against it Liam spoke about his mother, fearful for her, wandering over fields radiant with green, invoking her in this male and, for all its effeteness, urine-smelling place.

She was born in Moscow, grew up in the centre of the city, her father a university lecturer in ancient history. Their family was reasonably wealthy, their mother the youngest daughter of a landowner. She had two brothers, a cat, and lived in an apartment overlooking the church of St Saviour. Her mother played the piano and educated her children in books and music. Their house was full of books, books of glowing colour, books displaying ogres and Cossacks, princes and bears in purples and golds. It was the snow in Moscow Elizabeth Kenneally recalled though. She often spoke of it, standing at a window, the first flakes of winter coming, arbitrarily almost, telling her of the winter to come, a winter of thunderous fires, études by Chopin, books devoured beside a plate of steaming English buns.

When I first began noticing Mrs Kenneally I began listening to her, and in listening to her I pieced her life together like postage stamps. At these parties at the beginning of my adolescence she wore many dresses and it was perhaps these dresses that I recall more than her memories of Moscow – because she filled them so perfectly. Black dresses, dresses almost like crepe. Sometimes there were purple or white spots on them. She wore little jewellery, perhaps an inkling of necklace sometimes. But it was the dresses which made her and there in a room lined by mahogany floorboards, glass in her hand, expounding on some

6

aspect of the Russian Revolution she enthralled Irish people who had disowned all conflict, who wanted more than anything to be told they were right in disowning the human race.

When the Revolution came her family moved into the backstreets of Moscow. Typhoid raged and men wandered like smoke, ashen faces, ashen eyes. A priest fell dead outside their apartment one day and Elizabeth would never forget a faithful dog standing by him.

Even in war, she said, there is loyalty.

People in town adored her. She was better than the light opera, she told tales better than the Catholic press. Nuns more than anything admired her. She affirmed a world of pain, a world of persecution. They brought her jars of honey from the convent garden, gladioli, sweet peas and cakes wrapped in neat boxes.

They didn't realize she supported the Revolution, that she said over and over again that Russia had had to change and in changing it had altered one's way of thinking somewhat, that it changed one's attitude, that one realized there are no rules, nothing to obey, a chaos within.

Some ancient streak of aristocracy emerged in Elizabeth's mother – her family could be traced to the court of Catherine I she claimed – and when the lights went out in Moscow and men wandered like ghosts she asked for meringues, whereas most men were in want of bread. It was the terrible winter of 1916. A preacher stood at the corner saying that the world had come to an end. To all intent and purpose it had. The trams stood frozen, the Czar had gone. There was neither warmth nor bread and only fires lit the night, fires all over Moscow, a low moaning beginning like the stuttering of an elderly man near death.

They were brought to the country. Their father was left behind. There was a river, berries, birches, alder trees and in spring Elizabeth's mother went to the local hotel to play music. Her brother had grown somewhat and brought young women home. The Whites came to town, then the Reds. Elizabeth's mother entertained the Bolsheviks. One officer brought Elizabeth a doll. A doll with a black face and scarlet lips.

One day Elizabeth's mother disappeared.

A shot was heard that day at the local station where a young thief was killed by the Bolsheviks for stealing a rouble.

They were years of big men, men in long coats, moustaches, balaclavas. They came and assessed Elizabeth, a child, and let her be. Her father came from Moscow. She heard him speak of her mother, that it had run in her family, that she'd been a beautiful woman and an excellent pianist but like many Russian women her nerves were bad and forced to crack up she'd sounded a shrill note.

A peasant woman recalled having seen her wander in the woods collecting berries and a wood-cutter told how she'd spoken to him, having said she was like Mother Bear, fending for her children.

They were left in the country, she and her brothers, a woman left in charge of them, and their father came and went, wearing a beautiful tie. It was said their mother was sighted in a far-off place and to Elizabeth she would always be as a woman in a fairy story, gone into a distance of snow and rainbow sunsets and soldiers riding butter-milk mares. Her father, she said looking back, was a man of great authority. Even in those times he always bore the appearance of one who understood, who held things together. He came and went. His hair suddenly went white when the Revolution came. Somehow as prices soared he always had money to keep his children, guard them from hunger. Afterwards Elizabeth said she suspected he was a Menshevik. A woman looked after them, cooked for them, sang songs to herself as snow whisked outside. She missed her mother, missed the études, the books, the foreign recipes, especially the French meringues.

Her mother had had hair of almond colour, shot through with waves of honey and gold. She'd worn white, often with a suggestion, a bodice, a frail border, of emerald or lilac. Her

8

mother had mothered a piano like a friend. Finally her mother had cracked up, gone.

The peasant woman made hot beetroot soup in the evenings and one day when Elizabeth was eleven a young man, her cousin, came, took her to Moscow where huge crowds were rallying about a small fire-fly looking man. He took her on a train across Europe.

She had her doll. She lost her doll – at a border. It could have been any border. Her father was dead. The past was dead. Her brothers were gone.

They arrived in Vienna. She stayed there three months in a convent, was then sent to Ireland when the sound of machine guns was dying and she boarded at a convent on a street where a leader had just been killed emerging from mass. The order was a wealthy one and they sent her to college in time. She met Dermot Kenneally at a ball in 1933. He'd been a qualified doctor for over ten years, studying at a college from which a fellow student had been hanged. He began driving from his country practice to see her.

In 1934 she gave up her medical studies, married him, bore him a child. But living in a town bordered by woods there was always the memory of something undone, a doll left behind, marigolds not tended to, wine from Crimea not drunk.

'I have two brothers,' she said one evening, 'somewhere in the world. Peter and Ivan. They are beautiful men. They were beautiful boys.'

And I couldn't help associating them with a huge Airedale Liam had when small who escaped one evening out the gate, wandered about town all night, was found dead beside a dustbin in the morning.

Talking about his mother at school Liam wished her happiness. 'We are all bound into one, boys in Russia in 1918, boys in Ireland in 1949.'

St Patrick's day that year, the window by the stained glass maker was unveiled and a party was held to celebrate this fact in Liam's home. It had been a day of beating rain and we were briefly home, Liam and I, and so attended. The Bishop was there, a host of clerics, the maker of windows – in black as usual.

She was sipping rosé wine and in a voice that rose above the crowds quoted Teresa of Avila whom she had depicted.

> 'See that the lamp that you will bear
> Is filled with oil of virtuous deeds
> And since the soul great merit needs
> There must be this and more to spare
> For should your lamp go out while there
> Your tears will be of no avail
> So you must watch and never fail.'

The Bishop, a hilariously fat man, guffawed and quoted an Italian proverb to the effect that women are great talkers but always hide a double motive.

The artist said, 'Women, men, we are artists. The artist needs to create, needs freedom. I have put your window together, piece by piece, tinted glass on lead against light. Now you men of Ireland let us, the artists, put our truths together, our lives, our search.'

Afterwards I learnt that this lady was actually a devotee of St Teresa and had travelled many times to Avila.

'In a search for privacy,' Liam's mother said, 'in a search for a cell in which one can hide away for one moment and bring forth one's soul.'

The Bishop turned in conversation to a government minister that evening, and the secretary of the radical party then in power conversed with Mrs Kenneally.

He'd been a friend of Dr Kenneally at college. He'd taken to arms and in the civil war defended the Four Courts. He'd qualified as a lawyer, in the 1930s pursued a career in the I.R.A., still fighting for an integrated Ireland. He'd travelled extensively, been to Russia and to the States. Now he worked both as a lawyer and as a party spokesman, unflinching in his support for a united Ireland and a radical reorganization of

10

wealth. He was a tall man, his brown hair was turning gold and white. He held a glass of wine as though it was his due. He spoke to Mrs Kenneally about Mayo in winter where he rented a small cottage, going sometimes to light fires and walk and think on beaches devouring the huge Atlantic drifts of cloud.

It was like a winter's day, the rain still beating and men and women hurried into cars.

Eventually only Liam, Dr and Mrs Kenneally, the artist, the political secretary and myself were left. The maid came in with steaming coffee. We sat about the fire. Mrs Kenneally said that she must visit the extreme west of Ireland in the summer and the artist reminded her she was renting a house in Connemara and invited her. The flames died out, people waited. They waited as though for some remark which would fence them against the night. No such remark was forthcoming. The secretary rose. He said goodnight. He kissed Elizabeth on the cheek. 'Your skin smacks of wine,' he told her. Everyone laughed.

The remaining party of people streamed to the door.

The political man's mother lived in the neighbouring countryside. He was staying there that night. Farewells were said. The door closed. The artist who was staying the night turned before going to bed.

She said, 'I wonder what we've accomplished. Celebrating in a land of hunger and pain.'

Dr Kenneally replied, 'We've celebrated art, your art, your contribution to our national identity.'

The woman said, 'I have made a window so the light can come in a little better.'

She retired up the stairway. Dr Kenneally and Mrs Kenneally linked arms and went to bed. The maid, Liam and I cleared up.

I became fascinated, fascinated at being almost alone in a room where a chandelier sprayed the ceiling with trinkets of shadow, where a bookshelf ordered books, mainly brown or mustard colour. I chose one. It could have been like choosing

11

anything in the house, a leaf of mint, a tin of paprika, a piece of Dresden china. The book was an old college book of Dr Kenneally by the founder of the college he had attended, Cardinal Newman.

I opened it and read: 'This then is the plain reason why able or again why learned men are so often defective Christians, because there is no necessary connexion between faith and ability, because faith is one thing and ability is another, because ability of the mind is a gift, and faith is a grace.'

Liam touched me on the shoulder. I turned and saw a boy in a white sleeveless jersey, a radiantly white shirt, a tie of browns and yellows, thickly woven and thickly knitted under his chin, blond hair falling over his forehead. 'I'm tired. I'm going now,' he said. I wanted to ask him about faith, about the oak tree at the back of his house. I wanted to ask him why he had these things and I hadn't. I wanted to know something about purity. I suppose I reckoned that night that Liam was pure. What most people would lay down their mortal possessions for Liam had, a gift, a quality of seeing, of erasing mediocrity and putting himself only where there was a high-point.

'Goodnight,' I said.

The maid sat down with a cat white as a polar bear and put on a John McCormack record and I sneaked away into the night.

Ireland was officially declared a republic that Easter. Little boys in white shirts and long white trousers banged triangles as they marched about the town and Mrs Kenneally said, looking out a window, 'Vive la république. Long live a bloody eyesore.'

The tree in their garden flourished and that summer when the holidays came we returned to town.

One Sunday Dr Kenneally and Mrs Kenneally drove Liam and me to the country to visit the secretary of the political party who was residing with his mother.

The house was surrounded by yellow tulips. We drank tea on the lawn from white, blue rimmed cups. The mother was old and frail, knit together by a series of cardigans and stock-

12

ings. Mrs Kenneally for once was in white, albeit white patterned by crystalline spots.

'Now that we're a republic,' the political secretary said, 'we can send waves of reverberation into the universe.'

Mrs Kenneally said: 'This country is as a house divided. It is bound to fall.'

True to her promise to her artist friend she went west later in the summer. It was only for a day however but that day I'll never forget. Liam and I went too. We journeyed through some of the most beautiful countryside the world must know, where red petticoated girls stood with donkeys against a dust of purple and brown mountains. The car arrived, after refusing to travel certain roads. The house overlooked the ocean. The artist approached in a blouse of white and a skirt of grey. Her face was fat and her eyes huge like a generous cow's.

'Welcome,' she said.

It was a summer of lounging and lazing.

Drinking orange juice against a sea of evanescent blue the woman – looking in the direction of Tir-na-n-óg, the legendary land of youth – said, 'I have felt this pain in my right breast for a long time. Who knows but that my time as an artist is up.'

Later Liam said, 'We were privileged to know these people.'

I was.

There are always certain people whom you trust blindly and she was one, that woman. Her face, her eyes, her anguish. Towards the end of the summer we approached her, this time in a Dublin hospital where she was dying of cancer. Raised in the bed, indisputably ill, she said, 'I had two real relationships in my life. One with the sea. The other with Spain.' I thought of the dust roads in Castile and the house by the ocean and wondered about her art, stained glass windows in churches all over Ireland depicting the apostles, Christ, St Brigid, wondered why she didn't mention them, thought to myself that the real artist is an anonymous person whose art is unbeknownst to him.

She died in August.

13

She was buried on a grey day. Elizabeth read an oration. Her blonde hair frizzed at the hem of a black hat.

She quoted St Teresa.

> 'Not a friend was by his side
> When his cross he did embrace
> And to us came light and grace
> Through Our Lord the crucified.'

She wept a little, turned away.

I was in love with Mrs Kenneally from that day forth.

How do you know a winter is going to be bad? Winter 1949 to 1950 was terrible. It was like the war again but this time a war within. We were at school, aged fifteen. There was a need for something. We weren't sure what. And that winter Mrs Kenneally began having an affair.

The first wind we heard of this was at Christmas. Apparently Mrs Kenneally had taken leave of her senses and had begun taking short trips to Dublin to see the secretary of the political party.

She didn't come home once or twice. Her husband drove looking for her and found her with his college friend.

We were treated only to rumours. There were lemon boxes about in which Mrs Kenneally had brought home cakes from Bewley's.

The maid made magnificent Christmas cakes that year. The pantry flourished. But one was aware of discord. It shot through the household like forked lightning. There was Mrs Kenneally still beautiful, still awesomely beautiful. But her life had changed. She'd fallen in love. She had lost touch with something, an element of chance that bound her to a town of limestone houses, flourishing trees and languorous golf-courses. She had seen it again, through a keyhole, a way of life, Russia, her childhood, a place hurriedly left and always lingering.

'Think that a quietness of spirit hath a certain reward, that still thou art in the care of God, in the condition of a son, work-

14

ing out thy salvation with labour and pain, with fear and trembling, that now the sun is under a cloud but it still sends forth the same influence.'

Back at school we encountered a new prayer and Liam worried now, fears of last winter confirmed, left me often to walk over earth subsiding with rain.

It was those weeks, weeks of early January 1950, that I recognized that there was an area of psychic response in Liam to his mother, that her life was like a letter sealed in the white envelope of his, that he knew her and loved her, that now he waited as though expecting a calamity.

The man Mrs Kenneally was in love with was well respected. He'd never actually partaken in violence since the civil war but he had aided the violent revolutionaries of the thirties, men sneaking to England, leaving bombs like baskets of eggs in rubbish dumps. Though there was a streak of the Welsh ascendancy in his blood he was anti-British.

How come I knew how they made love? But I did. I did because I wanted to. My father was a pre-eminently respectable lawyer. I came from a pre-eminently respectable class but I wanted to be different, yes, I really did. She made love to, a man with whom she found physical intercourse revived something: snow, a boy's head of golden hair in Russia hallowed by a New Year's candle.

Dr Kenneally was a man of immense calm. Even at the school the world shook with the scandal. It was known in Irish political circles. It grew like a rare and rather irresistible gladiolus. One perceived it, the hand of God, a man and a woman in a small hotel in Dublin making love. Dr Kenneally treated this remonstration of passion like he would a covertly ill patient. He spoke to his male friend. The affair was disbanded. His wife was fished from the adultery. Life went on.

Nuns could have killed themselves. Their heroine had confused them. What about the train of gifts from convent to Kenneally home, the honey, the marmalade, the cakes, had they led to sin? The town reverberated with chuckles. Dr Ken-

15

neally, partially of Northern Protestant stock, held his head high. One could have given him a silver cup for bravery.

At Easter when we were at home it had gone. Primroses flooded the garden, a turtle trekked over the green.

Mrs Kenneally entertained an actor from a travelling theatre company and spoke with him about the plays of Middleton and Rowley.

We returned to school. The ground blazed with bluebells. A boy, alone, in white walked among them. I knew now that Liam would have to walk a long, long time before he encountered peace.

Her breakdown came gradually. She went to London in May, to shop, was found crying in Selfridges by a Catholic priest. He put her on board a plane. She stayed in Dublin two days. He wouldn't see her.

She returned home.

The river was cool and placid. May became June. Boys in white in the convent clashed triangles.

Madness too was like stained glass, inch by inch, colour by colour, crossing the sky. She cried out in the night but there was no one there to hear her. She'd known the softness, the regeneration of flesh for a while. Now it came, a chaos, a knowledge that a certain path could never be retraced, that loss was total and that chaos once known, was impossible to hold back. It came, it spread in her like a troop of military horses. It gathered. Sometimes in June when we were home she spoke of flowers, many flowers, a sky of flowers, flowers yellow like her hair, buttercups, yellow irises, primroses. She looked towards the river as though to a release.

There was no release. Dr Kenneally's friend was issuing press statements for his party. Dr Kenneally was trying to hope, holding back a world of madness. She spoke of a doll with scarlet lips.

I found the maid weeping in her pantry once.

Towards the end of summer, deformed mushrooms in the woods, they led her away. I became sixteen in December.

At Christmas there was no sign of her. She was in the mental hospital. No parties, no wine, no lips like petals falling from poppies at the height of summer. I didn't go to see her that Christmas. I couldn't bring myself to.

Liam read Tolstoy at school, he read Balzac, Flaubert, Zola. Sometimes it was as though he'd forgotten about it.

Before Easter we heard the news. Liam's father arrived and took him away.

They were still searching for her body when I arrived home for the Easter holidays. She'd walked into the waters of the river. People sat about the river bank, women from the poorer quarters of the town. The middle-class women of town said rosaries. The poor were silent. It was this river that gave them trout and pike and now they waited, knowing the worst, realizing that death is inevitable and that the death of one beautiful and rich in life is a death to be mourned more than most.

It was odd how I noticed signs of the spring, small children playing, primroses urging upwards beside an Elizabethan ruin.

It was approaching Easter Sunday when they found her. I couldn't bear to watch, but inadvertently turning to seek my own mother in the crowd I saw her body. I didn't want to. I didn't want to.

She was very pale, washed up in a black dress that clung to her like a possession. Her hair had become paler with death but no less gold. I wanted to touch her, her ear-lobe, a curl of her hair. I wanted to tell her it was all right, but a boy got there before me. He took off his black school jacket and not weeping, not wondering even, covered her in his black jacket, leaving himself clad in white.

Book Two

'WHATEVER BE MY AGE, whatever the number of my years I am ever narrowing the interval between time and eternity.'

The words of John Henry Newman could not have been further from the ears of young men beginning at University College Dublin in autumn of 1953. The world was full of trees and young women, young women sporting scarves, young women eager to absorb life, love and creativity.

We boarded in Haddington Road before being ejected for drunkenness. We then moved into an apartment in Monkstown, Dublin from which we could view the mail-boat slipping out to sea. Liam read a lot of Whitman, he was studying literature. I was studying law. Young men up from the country, not knowing about life but certain of one thing, privileged backgrounds.

Somehow the image of glass clings when I think of those years, still clings, the fashioning of a stained glass window, piece by piece across the sky. There were many images, each an iota of this window, each a colour, a hue, a variation, each making a journey towards a total truth. Although always bordered by the ramshackle, the city centre was chaotically beautiful and often you could spy an old man adept at astrology outside a flower shop, or a painter, gone in years, strolling by Stephen's Green, his mind a whirl of colours.

To this city came the virgin young of Ireland, bank clerks, civil servants, seamstresses. The tricolour lazed over all G.I.s sped through the town, in pursuit of uncertain goals and red sports cars flared by Grafton Street, reminding us that there was an élite, not us, the Anglo-Irish.

Boys going to college, we spent most of our time in Bewley's, mellowed by altars of buns, looking at the other occupants, old men, nuns, elegant women, under the aura of a certain stained glass window. One noticed the G.I.s with roses in their military lapels. One noticed the Americans, the Germans, the Dutch, the English. It was a city in which one had aperitifs in the Shelbourne lounge and waited, waited for what I don't know.

Liam in 1953 was a youth in a long coat, slapped about him like a nightgown, a loose strap on it, a fall of blond hair on his forehead, eyes like the eyes of one partaking in espionage and lips that understood the smoking of cigarettes, shattering clouds of smoke into the air.

I accompanied him in his search, a search that disowned college and trampled the city streets. We ducked in and out of cinemas. Greta Garbo was Liam's favourite, but there were fewer of her films out and he had to content himself with the best of Hollywood, *All about Eve*, *The Maltese Falcon*. Once in a pub he told me, 'I'm excited by this place. This city is like a handkerchief put together from bits of dirt. There's something to discover here.'

Our apartment was always a place to retire to, a languorous apartment holding a huge brown picture of Wales.

Liam wore white shirts in the evenings, he engaged himself in a rather off-hand manner, reading poetry, tracing the last movements of the mail-boat before it left the skyline, tipping over to Wales. He quoted Whitman often and left my ears singing with verses.

'I heard what was said of the universe
Heard it and heard it of several thousand years,
It is middling well as far as it goes — but is that all?'

I don't know why Whitman. I'll never know, another languorous male in a white shirt. I wanted to ask Liam then, before the charade began, why, why him, why the spontaneity, why the ultimate sense of grief and vulnerability?

Close following on Whitman were Irish names. Joyce was out of favour. He was too punctual, too ordinary. Liam loved Yeats, Synge and O'Casey. Each was romantic in his own way. Each told a story about the country in which we were now living, each aspired to Liam's sense of the universe. I couldn't exactly describe that attitude. All I know it was encapsulated

22

by Liam, hands in his pockets, outside a sky-blue Georgian door as leaves rustled like a piano concerto in Dublin, autumn 1953.

On November 25 we bought two big old bicycles and cycled into town each day, past Guinness carts and nuns with their gowns spraying in the wind. We careered past Trinity College, stopped in Bewley's. Breakfasts were generous, bacon and eggs, and we waited.

Soon fatigued of waiting, of casting poses, Liam dated some girls, young women like ripe tomatoes just released from Ireland's most prestigious convent schools.

We both dressed in black suits and dickie bows to escort a pair of Marys to a convent dress dance but soon discovered that it wasn't like that, we were drawn as the mail-boat seemed drawn in the evenings to another world.

Our first encounters with that world were through Christine Canavan, a girl just up from Limerick. She stayed with her grandmother up the road from where we lived and she was studying Greek and Latin at college. I chanced to speak to her one day on the corridor of Earlsfort Terrace. She was bearing a parasol, a big floppy lilac one bordered by moulded lace which her great-grandmother had borne, she claimed. She quoted Horace at me, hit me on the head with her parasol and walked off.

A strange girl I thought and then we encountered her again – in Bewley's. She'd come to feast her eyes, she declared, on the cakes and the parish priests. The priests here had all the variations of the rock buns, soft or mellow, hard or disgruntled. She was from a town of grey spires and grey pavements. It was occupied by priests, a myriad of them and a laity as hard as metal. Her family were wealthy. They'd imported wine from Spain and France for many years; she'd been educated in a convent where almond trees stood alongside benches where ancient nuns rested in the sun. She was certain of her history, certain of her background. But there was something less than certain about her, her hair auburn turning to brown, sometimes wildly red when light caught it, her freckles, her eyes that

23

watered into green and even on a bright November morning in Bewley's beseeched one.

Liam took to her, the aura of her childish laugh and she gladly played games for him. Sometimes she'd arrive in the evenings at our flat and we dipped over the gramophone playing Billie Holiday, lights swimming on the record, a voice serenely speaking of death, drugs and love.

Liam cooked a Russian meal one evening and we ate by candlelight, hot beetroot soup, Russian salad – potatoes, peas and chicory creamed in mayonnaise, floured with paprika – and shashlyk and she loved that. He'd bought wine – we others hadn't thought of it – and he began speaking of his mother. Christine was enthralled. The curtains juggled a bit. The sea was calm. He spoke of her blonde hair and her dresses and how she'd fallen in love, why he'd never know. Afterwards quite drunk, immersed in his own melancholy he quoted Whitman.

'There was a child went forth every day,
And the first object he look'd upon, that object he became,
And that object became part of him for the day or a certain
    part of the day,
Or for many years or stretching cycles of years.'

There was a silence after the music. The curtains were positively in tune with the mood, waved a bit, collapsed into silence. Liam led Christine home, leaving me to clean up the dishes.

Christine had one friend called Sarah Thompson, a Dublin girl whom Liam and I had noticed for the elegance of her movement and the richness of her blonde hair. We'd noticed her long skirts, lemon and white, her blouses, the way her shoulders seemed to arch. Somehow we were never with Christine when she was about so we were not yet introduced to her. It was Liam who first pointed her out. He had an eye for the unusual and Sarah was unusual. Among awkward adolescents she had the certainty of a society queen but we perceived her only with nuns and priests.

24

There was a lecturer in college who more than anything epitomized our first encounter with this new universe. She was about thirty-five, still wore her hair in a ponytail, generally wore black or long heavy purple coats. It was said of her that she'd once been summoned to Paris to discuss some point of philosophy with Sartre but we only saw her, always alone, walking a dachshund down the backstreets of Dublin where prostitutes rose like wraiths. Despite Sartre, Camus, Heidegger, the people she spoke about at philosophy lectures, she was inevitably and faithfully alone.

Why she should stand out I don't know. Both Liam and I were studying philosophy as a subsidiary subject and listened to the lady expound about Sartre and Camus.

'Look at a constellation of stars tonight,' she said during a lecture on Heidegger, 'and ask yourselves what's it all about, this makeshift journey between birth and death.'

True to form both of us did, we gazed out the window at a formation of stars over the Irish Sea. 'A child in the womb,' Liam said. Afterwards he fell in love with the philosophy teacher, followed her about town once or twice, divined her presence in pubs in conversation with an old fat lady in black or a long stringy cleric. That was all. Afterwards he went back to his books, looked at the faces of Sartre or Camus, asked for an explanation from them, was given nothing.

Because of Camus' interest in soccer we both began playing rugby again for a short while, taking to a pitch on rainy Sundays, flying after a ball with pale, fat, fleshy legs. We hadn't played the game since school. I had to relearn old tricks.

Christine Canavan came to see us one day. When the game was over we saw that Sarah Thompson was present. She was standing in a heavy fur coat beside a boy in a white suit. We had been playing Trinity College that day.

Christine made to speak to Sarah but by the time we emerged from the dressing-room Sarah had gone. 'That was Jamesy she was with,' she said. 'He's from Trinity. His father is an actor.'

And she salaciously mentioned the actor's name, an old man famous for playing Irish priests in Hollywood.

We walked to the bus. The sun was going down over the Irish Sea, cutting the heavens like an amethyst. It was a cold day, early in December. Christine was dressed in black, with a balaclava, a Russian.

'Soon I'll be going home,' she said, 'back to Limerick.'

'Aren't you looking forward to it?' Liam asked.

'No,' Christine said, 'no.'

Come Christmas we journeyed back to County Galway, the limestone town by the river which had spread out with floods. Something of the spirit of Christmas had revived itself in Liam's house. Aunts filtered through, old ladies from big houses beside little ponds of dahlias or begonias. He was of civilized ancestry, Liam was. If Catholic his relatives possessed a sense of courtesy, of independence. If Protestant they boasted extreme characters, a Methodist minister who ended up pursuing butterflies in Madagascar, a suffragette who'd been killed in a protest in England in the early part of the century, run over by a cab, an earnest pacifist, follower of Francis Sheehy Skeffington, the Irish socialist murdered by the British during the 1916 uprising. These were but some, a scattering of an intelligent and highly regarded family. Crackers were pulled in his house. The spirit of Christmas was engendered. The maid emerged with buxom fruit cakes. But Liam's father sat silently more than often, lamenting the dead and living with a nation constantly changing, constantly causing him anger.

Back in Dublin we spied Sarah Thompson after watching a Jimmy O'Dea pantomime one evening. She was with an old man, more than likely her father. We followed her through the streets afterwards, but lost her. Instead we encountered a group of gay drunkards, women with scarves of red check on their heads and we followed them to a Georgian house where they descended to a basement.

They were after hailing from McDaid's, home of the Irish literati. An old man with a goatee beard demonstrated that he had the biggest and finest bottle of whiskey. An equally ancient man, but one small and leprechaun-like, was urged to song and he sang 'She is far from the Land' in a voice that explored the destiny of the song and seemed to travel with it.

'Maith an fear,' a woman of forty said in Gaelic.

She rose, danced a jig with the leprechaun of a man, as a boy, pale, anaemic, blond, played an accordion.

The frail old man with the goatee beard reminisced about his friend Joyce. 'I met him in Paris once – you know he preferred sherry to port – and I said to him over sherry "Jimmy, what is your attraction to red silk handkerchiefs?"

'James Joyce said to me' – and the man breathed as though the whole world was listening – ' "They're my red flag. My symbol of prurience, of resistance." '

The leprechaun of a man sang again, drowning out the literary reminiscences, 'I have seen the lark in the morning' and a young woman wept.

The woman of forty was overheard saying to Liam, 'Leave her. She's pregnant. Some poet left her with a kid in the womb. Took the boat. I'm only afraid she'll put a bread knife through her stomach.'

It was a shocking remark. Conversation was becoming lewd. Someone threatened to pull a woman's knickers down just to see a little emblem of the Mona Lisa allegedly sewn onto them and we left, Liam and I, leaving literary Ireland for once and for all.

In the first weeks of the year Liam acted strangely. He was quiet, simple, recalcitrant in his brown coat. He strolled about town, spent less time in cafés. Always there was that stretch by the Green he loved, trees, green grass inside, flower shops decking the other side of the street.

Anglo-Irish ladies struggled about – literally on their last legs. They wore clothes like the clothes of a Victorian doll. Their hats always seemed more suited to scarecrows but they asked questions.

One wondered about fallen empires.

Liam's father came to Dublin for a day. We had afternoon tea with him in the Shelbourne. The first of the spring sunlight splashed the great orange building. Liam was wearing a sports coat and a tie. His father seemed to understand him more than anyone else. There was a quietness there, an ease. They flicked away ashes.

'I hope you're enjoying college,' Dr Kenneally said. 'It's a new university but not uninteresting for that. I think you can give a lot to it if you so wish.'

'Children of the élite,' Liam whispered one evening. 'Children of the élite.'

We were sitting in our flat, having finished a bottle of wine. There were plumes of red still in the glasses. Outside the evening showed signs of winter lifting. One thought of Galway at these moments, Liam's house, the garden, the river. One thought of school, the breezes that blew in from the Curragh. Liam's white shirt was open at the neck. 'O.K.,' I said, 'Children of the élite.'

'We're privileged,' Liam said, 'privileged. Privileged to money, class, more than anything manners.'

I realized what he meant but I wouldn't accept the difference. We had grown up on all the finest things this newly fledged society could give, good food, good schools, fine friends. What Liam was asking simply was: What are we going to make of it ourselves?

He took to his books more, took to being alone more, left me so that I wondered where I'd been going all these years, hanging around Liam. Before I could answer this question we met Sarah.

Christine was visiting us one evening. She had become friendlier with Sarah than she had hitherto been, so she'd arranged Sarah call for her. She called promptly. At 9 p.m. I answered the door. She was with her friend Jamesy. I asked them up. Outside was Jamesy's car, a big sports car, white with a black top.

Liam made coffee, introductions done. Sarah sat, admired

28

the view. She didn't say much. She sat like one used to being attended upon. We drank coffee. Liam said he was going to learn how to make buns. There were no buns that night, no cakes, silence almost. Sarah was the first to rise.

I led her and Jamesy and Christine to the door, Liam was silent afterwards. I didn't know whether in meeting Sarah he disapproved of her or liked her.

The next time I met her I was without Liam. She was after emerging from an Italian lecture.

'Someday I shall go to that country,' she said, 'it sounds lovely, Siena, Firenze. Yes I think I'd like Italy.' It was as though by thinking she was going to like Italy she was giving something to that nation. She'd been used to being looked after, tended to, waited upon.

I had coffee with her in the college canteen. She explained to me something about her background, or at least I picked it up, fragments, side comments. Her father was a doctor, lived in the most élite and the most exquisite part of Dublin, a big Georgian house. It had a garden, a summer house, steps on which her father had once been photographed with William Butler Yeats and Countess Markiewicz.

I wondered then, was she playing a game? She was very good-looking and that day she was wearing a pink dress like a child's. It had a border of lace about the neck. I checked the patterns, little blues and golds, for confirmation of an ultimate pattern. She was an only child, like Liam. I had brothers, albeit brothers gone, working for large firms in London. But she was out looking for something. Her home I was later to discover was one which reverberated with music, fine standards, high goals, but in a shabby canteen I wondered if Sarah had been neglected in some way, hadn't been given something children usually are given, the right to childhood, the right to innocence.

I bid goodbye to her on a long corridor. A nun passed us like a fat dolphin. I turned. I walked into an afternoon exhaling of spring.

Jamesy, Sarah, Christine called off and on in the jaded sports car and brought us to exhilarating destinations like Lough Dan or Annamoe, places stuck in the Wicklow mountains. Why they came so suddenly and so devotedly we'd never know. They arrived like a gust and did not easily depart. It was March and light breezes were blowing over the Wicklow mountains, turning the world to gold and emerald.

Sarah was adept at wearing scarves, chiffon scarves and silk ones often held by an antique brooch. Once, just once, she polished her nails with varnish. I noticed how frail her face was, almost like an old woman's, frail bones, a frail, dignified, arching nose.

Jamesy's car was a very suitable vehicle for these outings and later in the year we bedecked it with sprays of furze or heather. It was like a balloon in the wind, a *mardi gras* all on its own. It transported us and we transported it into a fantasy.

Jamesy was the odd one among us, a boy given to dressing in scarlet shirts, a very good-looking boy with a thin edge of a moustache. He was studying in Trinity, his secondary education having been completed off Hollywood Boulevard. His father was well-known and had acted alongside famous stars.

Now his family had returned from Hollywood back to their home in Dalkey. His father, a Protestant, his mother from an Anglo-Irish family in Connemara, they were a different species. Hollywood stars regularly rested at Jamesy's home. He was an oddity, a charm, a rare breed to be observed. He obviously wasn't sure what his relationship with Sarah was, but for the moment he was quite content to transport her friends on Sunday outings.

I confronted him in a café once. A rose was stuck in a wine bottle and he spoke about Hollywood, the time his father played Friar Tuck in a Robin Hood film and he started weeping when some English director called him an Irish slob. 'I'm of the gentry,' he'd told an uninterested Hollywood audience. 'Hollywood,' Jamesy said, 'a series of garages, a series of make-believe Roy Rogers, horses, whores, male and female.'

I'd never heard about male whores but I was open to finding out.

'You must come to my house some day,' Jamesy said as though addressing me alone but in fact he meant everybody, as I soon discovered, and we sprayed his house one day looking, looking at a portrait of an Irish soprano who'd once sung in Liam's home, looking at a Buddha straight from China, looking at a swimming-pool, a marble staircase, a collection of drink, liqueurs and brandy.

'Have some brandy from Auvergne,' Jamesy said waving a bottle. We succumbed, and Christine, presently a little tipsy, fell into the swimming-pool.

Oddly, Christine had taken back seat since Sarah had arrived on the scene and if you looked you would have perceived a certain degree of imitation. Christine wore gloves, black or grey, when Sarah wore them. Christine wore purple when Sarah wore blue. Christine wore hair combs when Sarah wore ribbons. Sarah more than anything initiated hauteur. She looked at everything as though it was significant. She initiated an era in our lives, an era of probing, of significance. We were all more than prepared to seek the truth.

Early in April we made off to a Catholic seminar being held in Meath about faith. The seminar was held in a Georgian mansion. Daffodils had already come. They greeted us, little hordes of them, a radiance of narcissi. Jamesy had gone along though he was a Protestant.

A French priest spoke about the Resistance. He spoke about one Simone Weil, a French lecturer in philosophy who'd died, starving herself in England as a gesture to the Resistance. He told how he'd fought during the war, the moments of fear, the moments of doubt.

'One waited for God,' he said, 'God never seemed to come. But one still hoped. One plunged oneself in the Christian virtue of hope.'

An American priest spoke of the poverty of negro ghettos in the States, he criticized his government for waging cold war

31

when its own poor were myriad. 'Americans,' he said, 'in fact people nowadays, like to believe they're saved from something. They call it the Iron Curtain. But they wear a belt of prejudice about them. What good are the suburban houses if we don't have an understanding of ourselves and the society we live in?'

Teilhard de Chardin was mentioned. Simone Weil was spoken of again, Teresa of Avila, Catherine of Siena, Charles Péguy, Marx, President Eisenhower, the Archbishop of Dublin. More than anything Gandhi was spoken of. Faith in pacifism, faith in the power of the spirit over the order of violence. Sarah got up and asked, 'What right have we to demand peace when violence is everywhere being thrown at people? Violence of the spirit, violence of the flesh.'

A nun said she'd just decided to leave her convent because Catholicism was a pretext for the bourgeois world, and a Protestant pastor from Germany reminded everyone that in the not too distant past men had to die for what they believed in, Dietrich Bonhoeffer, members of the Legion of Mary in Germany.

'All of us must pledge ourselves to something. A simple aspiration demanded of us by Christ. Never hide your light under a bushel.' A candle was lit and a nun sang Psalm 23.

There was an atmosphere as there might have been in France in Resistance camps. People slowly realized that there was a gathering of the aware. Slogans were being much abused. Capitalism, Communism, the Red Threat. Poverty was everywhere in Ireland while the Church handed out charity. A few people called together by a nun who lectured in theology affirmed the value of search.

People retired to the living room.

Jamesy was heard to ask, 'I wonder did Jesus ever sleep with anyone?' and someone played Glenn Miller on a gramophone. Sarah then rose, elicited silence while Canon de Pachelbel played.

Afterwards nuns, priests and a Protestant pastor departed while Sarah, Christine, Liam, Jamesy, myself were left.

Bach moved on the gramophone. Heat rose from the fire. Sarah said: 'I wonder what has brought us here?' And Liam said, life, at which time each of us spoke, a fragment about our lives. Liam said he'd had a mother who'd died in his adolescence and a garden. Christine said she'd acted as a clown in a school operetta once. Jamesy spoke about Hollywood, the long streets, the desert where pigmy snakes squirmed. Sarah spoke most wholesomely about certain music, certain cheeses, a certain way of life.

'My father,' she said, 'has spent all his life tending to the poor of Dublin, a surgeon. He fought in 1916. He wrote poems in Gaelic. As a boy he built aspirations about the dream of a republic. Now we have our house, our garden, a republic, and a confused and devastated realm outside.' The music stopped. I talked for want of something better about the leaves, the leaves at the end of our street at home and Liam ended off the evening with words from Whitman.

> 'Logic and sermons never convince.
> The damp of the night drives deeper into my soul.'

Afterwards there was a greater singularity about us. We seemed less a group, more driven by ideas.

Liam wore white jackets about town as it was spring and Sarah, Sarah, always elegant, was now motivated by a new austerity; she walked down Grafton Street as though being pursued by questions about faith and guilt and enlightenment.

After Easter we returned to a different Dublin, Dublin racked by pain for us of examinations. But it wasn't demented enough not to celebrate Liam's birthday on 17 May. Liam, Sarah, myself, made all the arrangements, certain cheeses, certain meats, certain bread but a strange and unexpedient thing occurred the week Liam turned twenty.

A school friend of Christine was drowned while boating in Galway city. Sarah accompanied her to the funeral. They arrived back just when the candles were lit and the curtains were rustling. Liam had made bacon and cabbage, a huge leg of bacon. He was poised over wine when they walked in, Christine's face tear-stained. The girls initially partook of the party. Then Christine wept. She wept because she did not understand why a girl of nineteen in far off Galway should subside into a lake of blue on an early summer's day. Yet I knew by looking at Liam's face that he understood. He understood the inequality of life and that that girl by dying at nineteen pointed to a moment immemorial when innocence was captured, never to be let go. He took hold of Christine, comforting her, trespassing upon her sobs, sharing, though not himself grieving, knowing somewhere from a long time ago that life pulls these punches like a scarlet handkerchief from a white suit.

I wanted to know more about these matters. But he resisted me, retiring that night when the celebrating crowd was gone, sleeping in a big bed, to be awakened early by the azure blowing in from the Irish Sea.

We each tended to our individual examinations and departed from a city grey where poets prowled like hungry dogs. Before getting the train home I chanced on a poem by a leading Irish poet in a pub with a high roof and stained glass windows. It read:

> Child, do not go
> Into the dark places of the soul
> For there the grey wolves whine.
> The lean grey wolves.

The poem appeared in some paper. I left it out of sight. There was a train to catch. Liam and I left this city of red brick, of uneasy mannequins, of woodbine cigarettes and brimming hot cross buns on a June day in 1954, knowing it would not be long before we returned. Christine had gone home. Jamesy was helping his parents entertain for the summer, but Sarah had gone south, to be a children's nurse in Florence, and in the course of the summer I could see that Liam was thinking of her, fluff flying by in the Galway air. Nothing had really registered between them, blond hair yes, a relaxation in white, white shirts, white dresses, but now I could perceive further. Lounging on a red and green striped deck chair in his garden I wondered did I perceive that Liam was in love?

We went to the Galway races with Liam's father, we went boating on the river, we fished, we swam and then one day like a tramp Liam up and went. He caught a train from the station where marigolds were subsumed into the August light. He travelled by day and night until he reached Florence. I had a postcard from him.

'August 23, 1954. Arrived.' I detected on it the cathedral and baptistry in Florence. I wondered, I waited until he came back, drinking wine and then he came, flushed and brown and he told me, told me about the journey through France, his first sight of grapes.

'It was so beautiful,' he said, 'women tending to grapes as though they were the genitalia of men. I'll never forget that sight. I rose, looked through a window, wondered is this my life?' And afterwards I couldn't help wondering was this his life? A young man, for ever drawn south, towards the sun, towards a way of life, easier, more creative.

But in early September listening to Liam I knew it all, his arrival, his walking with Sarah through streets glowering with heat in the day, at night lit by trattorias like candles. 'There was Piaf,' he said, 'Perry Como, Palestrina, whoever you desired. G.I.s, whores, priests.

'We drank capuccinos. We feasted on them. The leaves were turning brown – like – like – ' and this I will never forget ' – like a Caravaggio. It was excellent.'

They'd probably not even touched once. But such was love then, an outward gaze, a world one would have built again, if one could, a world of innocence.

They returned from the bogs, they returned from the parochial hall doors. They came from Clare and Monaghan, back

35

to college. Young girls, young men, they returned to a city now where skies flourished over grey suits, searching bicycles, little men with eyes like Lenin who searched ledgers for a statement on life. 'You are young once only,' a nun stated on the corridor in Earlsfort Terrace and each of us heard it, me, Liam, Sarah, Christine and the news was reported to Jamesy at Trinity.

We were back, shunting of trains still in our ears, far off places, bogs, blues and the whisper of geese in the night. Christine was back from her aunt's place in Leitrim. She'd spent the summer feeding geese, tending to sheep, watching Atlantic skies wash in huge mistaken clouds. Her identity seemed somewhat shaken by the summer.

Liam, Sarah moved through the corridors of Earlsfort Terrace, quiet, Liam with hands in his blazer, Sarah often quite ridiculously holding a handbag, eyes ahead. It was as though the handbag both provided an ultimatum and guided her. She'd changed.

Jamesy in Trinity looked lost, a young man who'd become taller over the summer and me, I too, had changed.

Like Lord Nelson over Nelson's pillar I watched as a city engaged in its daily business, as the poor became poorer and mouths opened, singing an anthem like 'Starvation once again.'

'I dreamt about the tricolour last night,' Sarah said one day, 'I dreamt that I was caught by it as though by a huge bird, that it had enfolded me and that I was trying, trying to break free from it. I woke. I was sweating. There was blood on my hands!' Our eyes glazed over her handkerchief-pale hands to detect blood but saw only the vulnerability of untormented fingers.

We went to mass and listened to priests drone in Latin.

One afternoon for want of something better to do we all trooped off to the airport to catch sight of a visiting thirties movie star, all except Jamesy. His father having acted in Hollywood he was used to it all. We watched her through binoculars descend from the aeroplane. She was ushered into the airport lounge, holding back from camera-men, hiding herself against the flashes of their cameras. We noticed her parrot-red lipstick,

36

her eyes outlined in black merging into a puppet-pale face. For one moment she raised an eyebrow and it was as though we photographed her in our minds, a thirties film star, wandering into the fifties, frigid, performing foolish gestures of retracting fame – too late.

These were the minor moments of escape. A more major effort to shake off shackles occurred later in the autumn.

We hit the town in the evenings, going dancing.

Liam and I were living in another part of Monkstown, in a flat overlooking the sea. Earlier in the autumn Liam had read Rilke, Rupert Brooke, Francis Ledwidge, seating himself in a corner distant from everything but the sound of boats withdrawing and arriving at the harbour. Now however we indulged in the few lighted places in Dublin, dance-halls with a few seedy coloured lights and interiors jammed like cattle-marts with country bachelors.

Christine above all loved these places, dancing with country bachelors, egging them on, exacting proposals of marriage from them. One man told her he had ten heifers in Galway and did she wish to marry him. Christine threw her stole in the air, said no and walked off.

One could detect Sarah and Liam dancing but they didn't dance to the music of Glenn Miller or Benny Goodman. The music that united them was elsewhere, the music of flourishing oaks and odd primroses. Sarah was acquainted now with all aspects of Liam's past, the peas in spring and the leeks oddly separated in the patch of earth under the oak tree.

Christine often noticed them lingering with one another after a dance was over, a fateful stop-over, a cup of tea, a sherry consumed with excessive patience. She couldn't figure out the rationale of these moments. They defied the spirit of a group. Yet nothing yet was certain; there were only momentary fears. The music played on, Christine often drank too much, raising her arms like an old lady at an Irish funeral and Jamesy, his eyes liquid and over-brown from drink, danced with the most elegant women in sight, women whose virtue was in peril.

37

Certain women had taken to the streets of Dublin, shouting about cardinals in far off places. *The Student Prince* came to town and even the flower-sellers on O'Connell Street seemed to waltz to the rhythmn of 'Drink. Drink. Drink.'

There was talk again of the North, always a far off reverberation and a boy from Roscommon declared on Earlsfort Terrace one afternoon that Ireland had to rise from the mire, a phoenix reborn, but the small farmers still flocked from Mayo to London and the poor of Dublin looked knotted into their pain. Sarah spoke of the need to change, the need to ameliorate the condition of workers. She spoke of the slums of Dublin, places she'd visited on evenings walking alone. But no one listened.

Rain came in November like a deluge, and one evening Jamesy's father threw a party.

Jamesy's home lay outside Dublin, a two storey house by the ocean. It stood upon rocks and always at night the sea seduced, distant lights, noise. One was led to the sea as though to an exterior effect of the house. It assembled lights, colours, an astonishing medley of sounds. Ultimately it told one something of Ireland, this ancient country, always bordering on sea, on sky, an unclear bond between it and other countries.

Music gently eroded the soft breezes the evening of the party, conversation rising and falling near the window-sill, women in black, penitential, the menfolk like bumble bees to a man, bellies swollen with drink.

A lady, Protestant, spoke in an arch voice about her acquaintance with W. B. Yeats. 'The Greatest Irishman,' she said, and a raucous Dublin accent called out, 'What about Eamon de Valera?'

'A stringy French bean,' the Protestant lady issued over a liqueur and the Dublin man said, 'Well we had Matt Talbot and Sean McDermott,' confusing an alcoholic martyr and a young hero, 'And you call your man Yeats great.'

Whereupon the Protestant lady marched to the window, looked upon the ocean and cried as though to the Hill of Howth opposite, 'And great art beaten down.' The Dublin man, an actor, began singing 'Kelly the boy from Killane' when a Hollywood starlet walked in past the swimming-pool, a little black cape about her wasp-like shoulders. She smiled, hiding a multitude of complicity under the umbrella of her smile. A journalist veered towards her, a lady journalist and nearly fell in the swimming-pool. Benny Goodman began to play up, saxophone music from New York troubling the night, the moon that had just emerged from the clouds, standing above Dublin bay like a Roman sovereign.

Mrs Nesbitt, Jamesy's mother, held a glass of sherry as though she was outstretching an antique thimble. She stood. People looked at her. She had certain airs, graces, blown at her from the Twelve Pins in Connemara. Daughter of an Anglo-Irish family, many of her relatives gathered, astonishing ancient men like jaded Irish wolfhounds, ladies from the mansions of Connemara or Wicklow, lichen virtually grown into their manners, their chins uneven, chins that told of an iron dominance of Ireland for 900 years.

Jamesy's mother spoke to Sarah, Christine in that order. She spoke to Liam, to me, civilized conversation with Jamesy's newfound friends. Sarah would have been impressive, Sarah in white, Sarah holding a handbag. The mixture of coquette and saint.

I perceived Liam in a black blazer and white shirt, the shirt singularly white, his hair the colour of daffodils before opening, green upon yellow. Odd moments I looked and he was there, totally there, there like the oak tree of old, holding out somehow, against time. He was totally present that evening, the sound of a New York saxophone edging in upon his silhouette against the darkening Irish Sea.

Someone entered and spoke of snow.

Someone else entered and told about a hungry protesting mob he'd seen.

A woman with a yellow scarf dotted with red still on her head entered, one flake clinging to her scarf, and her Anglo-Irish voice rebounding in the room, telling of a Catholic group

39

she'd seen in O'Connell Street, bearing flame and pictures of prelates behind the Iron Curtain.

A parson with a voice rich as British vegetables spoke about the *I Ching*.

A dotty old professor muttered about Archimedes.

The film star had her picture taken.

As if as an afterthought Jamesy's father announced it was his birthday. A birthday cake entered as though on a magic carpet. It was in fact borne by a maid. The Hollywood starlet got upset, began crying. A birthday serenade was sung.

Sarah sat by the swimming-pool discussing Troubadour poetry with a young academic from Cambridge. Christine and the Dublin actor were singing 'Carrickfergus' in a corner. Liam was moping about, fingering porcelain, china, holding it as he had held little snails wrapped in their nuggets of shells as a child. The parson was loudly telling ghost stories, witches, ogres, poltergeists seen in Wicklow, when I discovered Jamesy with his trousers down making love to an older woman.

First time I'd ever seen anyone making love. I reckoned that evening it was a Protestant, Anglo-Irish thing to do. I'd drunk too much. I was aware of friends floating, each on their own journey. I now knew the illusion of togetherness between us but I didn't wish to think about it. I knew the unalterable gap that lay between people.

The moon re-emerged and the Hollywood starlet could be seen standing on rocks, holding a glass of rosé, looking towards the Hill of Howth as though to Hollywood's lost illusions and Jamesy's father spoke of Hollywood, time he'd played an Irish priest in a film and a young American actor entered the confessional and said – the lines weren't in the script – 'Father, I don't make love. I masturbate.' A woman who looked like a wedding cake, layer upon layer of her, sang an aria by the piano and Jamesy's mother in the absence of Jamesy, talked of Connemara, the mountains, the beauty, days on white horses among rhododendron bushes.

Someone addressed Jamesy's father. 'Mr Nesbitt, how come

40

you never played Hamlet, always Polonius?' whereupon Jamesy's father recited the last lines of Othello, forgetting the very end, lapsing into Molière, then standing on a table, drunk out of his mind, taking down his trousers, waving them in the air, crying. 'A glass of wine, a loaf of bread – and thou, thou, thou.'

No more was seen of the Hollywood starlet. People presumed she'd taken a boat to sea. The parson said what Ireland needed was the royal family. Jamesy's mother had found a titled gentleman among the crowd, a relation of the Queen of England. Her husband was wandering around in his knickers, his balls bulging and his knickers huge like a child's nappy. An English lady screamed that she'd seen a mouse and a leading Irish poet entered, accompanied by his cohorts, danced with a rounded Anglo-Irish lady, stuffed himself with English cheddar, accused everyone of being 'a shower of fucking bejayus wankers,' put an arm about Liam's shoulders and said, 'I can tell you've got sense.'

Liam walked away. He was quite drunk. I could suddenly tell his head was swimming with drink. His eyes were glazed. He made for the swimming-pool and jumped in. There was horror. People stopped. Jamesy's father who had fetched a photograph of himself with Lady Gregory was silenced.

One could see that Liam had disappeared to the bottom of the pool. I knew what was happening, recognized the glaze in his eyes from a long time ago. I jumped in, in my clothes.

I caught Liam. I knew that he was trying to drag himself down, that again it was a long time ago and a woman was weighting herself down to the bottom of a river. 'Liam,' I screamed. I caught him by his blond hair, tugged him up. His shirt was torn half off. He lay unconscious by the pool. A man gave him artificial respiration. Sarah knelt beside him. She didn't touch him. Just looked.

And afterwards, long afterwards when Liam was asleep in an upstairs room I saw floating in the swimming-pool a portrait

41

of a well-known Irish soprano with carnation-red lips who had once sung in Liam's home.

There was never any mention of this event in the weeks afterwards. It went untold, a dogmatic silence surrounding it and words fewer between us.

As it turned out it was a winter full of light and come spring we set off to the mountains on bicycles, surmounting the Dublin mountains and the Wicklow mountains, stopping at pubs where Sarah entertained young Dublin workers out trekking for the weekend with ballads in Gaelic.

Only Christine complained, lazy laconic Christine who hated our ambition and was interested only in drink and sloth, sitting in pubs gossiping with farmers who had moustaches growing out of their nostrils. Sarah sang her way through Wicklow, songs about trees falling before Cromwellian invaders and forests laid to waste by the Cromwellian enemy. She sang of coves and monasteries in the West of Ireland, places her father once went to with British countesses to learn Gaelic.

Liam climbed the furthest, cycled to Olympian heights, the first shadows of spring arriving and young men, he, I, Jamesy, shedding jumpers for shirts and shirts for chests, nubile and tense.

Yes, go to Wicklow sometime, travel these paths, fairy places, places in Grimm's and Hans Christian Anderson's stories, and think, unsolemnly of Christine, fattish maiden pushing behind, Sarah, slender butterfly pushing ahead, Jamesy always in tow, never pushing too hard, Liam flying ahead, beautiful against time, possessed of a quality of looks that turned the heads of farmers' wives and often upset munching cows.

Then there was me, Sean McMahon. Without me they wouldn't exist. One puts them in an envelope, ancient photographs, forgotten nicknames. Sometimes my children ask me, a middle-aged lawyer, what it was like to be young. I tell them lies. I say it was great. And it was. It was for a while.

The first time I realized they were sleeping together was at Easter.

It came suddenly, night of Holy Thursday. I walked home from the Pro-cathedral to Monkstown, ignored buses, clear on some course. When I entered the house I made little noise. I climbed the stairs. Tchaikovsky played within. *The Sleeping Beauty*. I opened the door. Inside was a lighted room, the *Saturday Evening Post* open on a sofa. I engendered some noise. Then I was aware – swift as incense was thrown in the Pro-cathedral that evening – that there were people in the bedroom.

Someone, more, rushed for clothes. Minutes later Liam emerged, immaculate in a white shirt, white trousers. Then came Sarah. She smiled.

I'll never forget her smile, a struggling little smile. More in the nature of a smile on a Dresden doll. But still a smile. Sarah left that night, catching a taxi home, as though bent on some errand which she suddenly remembered.

I perceived Liam staring at me, eyes gone from blue to green and a clarity about them which cut through me and took me back, shed covered in ivy, a trail by a yard into a garden, a garden filled with growth.

He didn't speak about it. I didn't wish to ask him.

I stayed up that night, drank tea bought in Smith's of the Green and encountered a mouse who looked at me with know-ledgeable sadness and went away. I put it down to baby-sitting, time Sarah guarded her aunt's young children and Liam stayed in the house with her. They'd been reading a lot, Dostoevsky, Sartre, Camus, Heidegger, Kate O'Brien, Edna Ferber, Evelyn Waugh, but I reckoned it was D. H. Lawrence, that wily Englishman, who did the trick, united them one even-ing as they sat over a fire reading *The Rainbow* in carnal know-ledge. I had to be clear in my mind about it. I had to put things in order. I had to know, to expect the best of them. I wanted them to be happy. I wanted them to be enduring. I imagined Sarah's aunt's home, filled with portraits of elegant Irishmen, and wanted them to know that at least they had the gaze of heroic people upon them, poets, revolutionaries, those who'd bound the fate of a nation into their everyday lives.

The face of Sarah Thompson haunted me that Easter, at cermonies in our home town, over Easter lunch, a face of a blonde headed girl in a house full of Waterford glass and beaming pianos, saying grace with her parents or meditating as an afterthought on the tale she'd heard in church of the risen Christ mistaken for gardener.

The leaves were coming at the end of our town, true to form; old men stood outside the men's club and the odd donkey and cart went by, heading to bog-land.

I stood again outside Liam's home, a child, expecting Liam's mother to re-emerge and say it had all been a fantasy and that she'd never really gone mad or killed herself but was back and speaking again of Moscow and the ikon in a certain church which frightened her, an ikon displaying a virgin who seemed to have a fungus growing underneath her nose.

Back at college people lazed over books.

Liam and Sarah slept openly with one another or at least admitted it to me – and summer came early, a zenith of blue days whereupon we boys, Liam and I, cycled to town, motioning through space and time on three speed bicycles.

We parked them in Johnson's Court and indulged in bacon and eggs in the mornings in Bewley's – flying first past the gates of Trinity – and as days became warmer we journeyed first to the Forty Foot and swam early in the morning before the gulls rose like white streamers into the blue air. We swam naked, after encountering an ancient Dublin Neptune, belly below him like a cave and balls like saplings.

In Bewley's under a stained glass window, hair grazed with sunshine that had succeeded in entering the glass, Liam told me, 'To be in love is like ironing a white shirt. You take something of yourself off, wash it, then iron it to perfection.'

Oddly enough he was wearing an open-necked white shirt that morning.

Sarah, on the other hand, belied nothing in her manner, talking still about Camus and the war, looking into the Dublin sky and saying things like, 'It's got to change.' What had to change one wasn't sure, the sky, the clouds, the universe? Her meanings were troubled, succinct, often without irony. Sarah Thompson was going to alter the course of civilization.

Christine came to see us once or twice early in May. The sun was shining, the sea a gorgeous blue and she, a girl in a pink dress, recognized change, couldn't account for it, didn't know whether it lay with the picture of the wilted Lady of Shalott or the Japanese water-colours or elsewhere. She looked about, picking up napkins, paper flowers, antique spoons, watching a pattern in the carpet suspiciously. Then suddenly she turned from the window, her hair lit by sun, looked towards Liam, and I in my innocence knew her for what she was, a girl in love.

Sarah came and cleaned cups, saucers for tea. Always cups were shining when she served. There were just the three of us in the evenings, Liam, Sarah, me, a window open, the sea calm and conversation lapping like tides of the Irish Sea.

They slept with one another as I read. I read Tennyson and Rupert Brooke in those weeks, never my law books. There was always music. It didn't matter to them that I knew. The realm of the flesh was as every other realm. One – to be safe – guarded yet not over-protected. The knowledge of their intimacy was easy to me. I accepted it – at first.

May 17 was Liam's birthday and the anniversary of the funeral of Christine's friend. To celebrate Liam's birthday we all trooped off to a night club. Young men in tuxedos wearing carnations, women variously dressed, Sarah in a hamster white outfit, dress and cape, and emerald earrings in her ears that were well shown off with her hair tied up.

The night-club was a tiny, secretive place, known to diplomats and actors. Tonight we were to have a spree, Liam having been handsomely funded by his father for the evening and Jamesy, Jamesy as always with money. He had a red car now and we drove up to this place, situated as it was near the river Liffey, bodies squelching bodies and dresses erasing the neat folds on dresses. Christine had on a dress with an apple blossom sheen and reeked of lilac perfume. She looked pretty, dandy that evening.

An old negress was dancing with an old negro. 'Red roses for a blue lady' was playing. An orchestra who looked like overgrown boy-scouts in tuxedos belching away into saxophones. Beside us a British millionaire sat with his wife. They were having a row and the row seemed to spread as the old negro and negress, diplomats from an African country, became involved in argument in the course of the evening, and the negro lady began singing out loudly 'The last time I saw Paris' whereupon the orchestra picked up the tune and we all danced, Liam with Sarah, Sarah with Jamesy, Jamesy with Christine, me with Sarah.

French cigarettes were consumed. French wine.

'It smells of the Camargue,' Liam said, though he'd never been there, 'fires left after the gypsies.'

He was staring intently into a glass of wine. I wondered what he'd do if a time came when there was no money, no Sarah, no white starched collar, no black dickie bow.

Jamesy was dancing with a Dublin senator's wife and the music eased to blows and whispers about Paris, Berlin, New Orleans while we became excessively drunk and Irish people argued in the background about politics and the African woman broke a glass of wine on the floor before marching off, weeping about her husband's decision to come to this hell-hole, her bottom rising with indignation and hurt like a turkey's.

An Irish senator was reciting the proclamation of 1916 into his whiskey while his wife danced with Jamesy.

I sat with Liam.

'How do you feel?' I asked him.

'Well,' he said. 'Well.'

'Are you having a happy birthday?'

'Lovely.'

He seemed so still, so silent, like a water-lily just opened on the river behind his home when we were children.

'Do you hear it?' he asked.

'What?'

'Music,' he said. 'Music from another planet.'

I couldn't, I said. 'Let's dance,' he said.

He led me to the floor and danced with me, and I, humiliated, turned to Christine, grabbed her from a conversation with an ageing, but elegant, poet, danced with her while Liam took Sarah from Jamesy, bowed his head on her shoulder, kissed her neck, squeezed her thighs and waltzed to an American civil war song.

I often wondered about Jamesy's real feeling towards us. He'd been drawn into our forces by an invitation from Sarah. He followed her, never sure of his relationship with her. Now he stood, watching a rite. Christine too stopped, watched, was suddenly aware they were lovers. I could feel the hurt in her, quick as a sting of a wasp when one was a child halting one, disturbing her. She reached for me not knowing what she was reaching for, knowing she'd been rejected, not wanting to believe it, realizing that it was over, this dream of communion and simplicity between the sexes, that here in a Dublin nightclub Liam Kenneally and Sarah Thompson were bonded in the kind of relationship that had driven his mother to the bottom of a bottomless river.

Christine pulled at my shoulders. 'Let's go,' she said. She knew in those moments the essence of the last weeks, their signs, their foreboding. She realized she'd been deceived by this lack of physical intimacy and like an eagle wounded against the sun, wanted to scream until her outcry was heard and her body was assuaged and melted into another.

I was safeguarding the keys of Jamesy's car and so we made to it, opening it, driving off into the dawn. I made love to Christine that night. Beside the sea at the Forty Foot in Sandycove, my first time, hers, in the back of a petroleum red car under a petroleum dawn. She came like a bird, wounded, frigid from pain, screamed a little. I pained her. I was the rugby player, the young athlete, Pan. She was the female, the object.

47

I wanted to hurt her very much and she wanted the tenderness of hurt. She lay afterwards.

I walked to the sea. An old man no longer ashamed of his belly was emerging from his early morning swim. Dawn was coming over the Irish sea, a boat emerged into sight. I addressed the mermaids, the ocean, the neglected and forgotten anchors, took out a French cigarette and sucked it until I thought of the aftermath of gypsy fires in Camargue.

Jamesy had had to walk home alone that evening. Sarah and Liam had taken a taxi home and Jamesy without his car, without his keys, with his shirt open against the ocean, had had to walk past the flat, place where Liam and Sarah were united in love.

Relationships were clearer in the next few weeks. Liam and Sarah held hands. Christine linked my arm and Jamesy, Jamesy uncomplainingly drove us in his red car, a chauffeur now who'd lost his direction. They were weeks to be driven too, weeks of sun, of painlessness. In Iveagh Gardens in Earlsfort Terrace we perched under a larch tree while someone distantly whistled 'Don't sit under the appletree with anyone else but me' and Christine and Sarah looked like country maidens, stored up in summer dresses.

Her sexuality was strange to me, Christine's, its images, its phrases, its language. She spoke of the war, the school she boarded at as a child though her parents only lived a stone's throw from this place, storms ruffling the Shannon, nuns going hysterical in the night, whining like sirens and all the time bombs falling abroad and she a young girl of an upper middle-class Limerick family in a neat brown uniform, a neat brown suit on days off, with a medallion of Maria Goretti, Italian child martyr, about her neck.

Her parents were of an old merchant family and in childhood, despite the fact she lived in a big house in Limerick, she had endless crazy aunts and uncles to visit in County Clare during school holidays. Her parents would bring her in a horse and trap to old crumbling houses where the apple-trees never

48

prevailed beyond crab-apples and spinsters and bachelors waited like the eyes in old stone dragons, never moving, never acknowledging anything, never realizing anything.

Christine and Sarah both had lovers now. Unusual among Irish girls for the time – I suppose they too were unusual, two girls in summer dresses occasionally wearing huge Ava Gardner type hats to keep the sun away and to establish the time, the place, the reality of Maytime and student days and the odd quotation from Horace.

Christine had all but abandoned her studies; love was enough. This carnality among the grass, the thistledown, the odd patterns of sun. I wanted to tell her it was temporary but she would not have believed it; it was the beginning and the end for her, a time, head back on the grass, when my body or for that matter any other body would have sufficed.

We travelled to the Hell-Fire Club one evening, Sarah, Liam, Christine and I, all in Jamesy's car. It was late May and mild and we looked at the city from the seat where young Dublin bucks had once celebrated with Satan and diced their lives, loves and estates on a game of baccarat. The city glowered a little below us, neon merged into white glow and the sea coming close to the city, frightening it.

Christine said 'I'm glad I'm here, not elsewhere. Glad I'm alive, not dead. Glad that I have my life before me, that's all that matters, that I'm alive and it's only starting.'

Sarah spoke about Erik Satie, about creativity, the forces of the fingers behind a piano.

Liam said, 'It's a shame the whole world is not with us.'

I said that life was like cards, one wins, one loses and Jamesy, only Jamesy, spoke of the devil who'd once been known to frequent this place, Hollywood, Dalkey, his heritage, Anglo-Irish merged into the mores of the film world.

'I was born into a heritage I had no right to,' he said, 'One can only fail having been given lies or succeed totally, break away from it, create anew.'

Figures walked away, Liam with Sarah, Christine with me

and only Jamesy stood at the highest point, hair blowing and the petals of a rose freeing themselves from his lapel. It was drawing towards the close of the school year and one boat from Trinity set up the Liffey seeking some lost Parnassus, young men in white rowing away.

Jamesy's father had a small dinner party one evening to celebrate the visit of an American film director. Afterwards we arrived, Liam, Sarah, Christine, myself, on Jamesy's invitation. We danced. We drank. Again there was a moon over the ocean and white caterpillars of surf outside.

The American film director spoke of Tennessee Williams. 'A modern Orpheus,' he said, 'singing of man's lost love.'

Django Reinhardt played 'Moonlight in Picardy' on the gramophone and we young people drank the best wine, indulged in the most elaborate liqueurs, drinking and feasting as though we were the rightful heirs to this place and these delightful moments. Gradually directors, actors, parents sidled off and we were left there, dancing couples, Sarah, Liam, Christine, me, when a boy came to the top of the marble stairs, drunk, dishevelled. Jamesy. He had a drink in his fist, his shirt open, and suddenly, all of us, like butterflies in winter, froze, realizing something was wrong.

Slowly the boy walked down the stairs, picking each step. We knew him to have been crying by the tears in his eyes and it suddenly occurred to us that none of us arch Catholic children had noticed that this Protestant boy had been missing from our company, albeit for an hour. When he came to the final step he stopped, raised his glass high as it would go and suddenly, just suddenly, threw it until it smashed against a sparrow's egg blue wall.

'You've used me,' he said simply. 'You've used me.'

That was the end of Jamesy. He effectively dropped out of the cabal that evening late in May and it made things easier, romance and all that, the undisturbed violin tune of a blind musician on Aston Quay, the humming of a charwoman in a

50

Georgian house filled by light, the astral simplicity of birds perched on an electric wire in a Georgian square in Rathgar.

A few days before going home after examinations I walked into the bedroom to find Liam lying naked on a bed and I wondered if this was what it had come to, the fine schools, the sleeveless jerseys, the photographs of laconic young First World War soldiers and the leaves, the leaves on grey. I told Liam that I was going to cycle by the sea but he just muttered something and I cycled off alone, leaving a sensual youth on a brown eiderdown, sun pouring in on top of him and his blond head on a sparkling pillow, thinking, thinking of his lover, his life, his youth and the boundless days ahead when one could link the arm of a blonde girl in a black satin dress and escort her into a world of bright lights and grateful eyes.

Liam stayed in Dublin for the summer. I went home.

Christine came to stay with cousins in a neighbouring village and I joined her, sitting with her by the river Shannon, eating brown bread and honey, basking under the gaze of country aunts who reckoned we were a proper combination and that I was heading in the right direction, to the legal profession. Ireland was a place where law was one thing and actuality another and those who could disentangle the connection in their virgin nation reckoned to be brilliant, hallowed even. So a variety of Christine's aunts festooned the way to the altar for us that summer.

She stayed three weeks, weeks in which she even became dignified. The fields were full of corn by the Shannon when she left, an odd poppy embroidered into the riot of harvest yellows and golds and at the station she looked at me with a beseeching look which said, 'Please don't forget these days, the solemn afternoon teas on the big oak tables out of doors, the flies in the larch trees and the gleaming golden knockers on country houses.'

The train pulled off.

I knew I no longer loved her. Who or what I loved now I wasn't sure but not the Limerick girl forever uncertain, forever beseeching, forever, despite carnality or kisses, lonely as she had been as a child, relinquished by her parents and left to have nightmares about bombs falling abroad and nuns wheezing with virginal complaints.

A funny thing happened that summer which I learnt about later on.

In early June, fed up, left-over, Jamesy encountered a young Dublin girl while sitting on the steps of Trinity. She was working in a factory but had ambitions to become a model and talking to Jamesy she discovered he had a rich, upper-class accent, touched by the Pacific coast of America, that he was good-looking and dressed well and furthermore that he had a lovely laugh which that day reverberated throughout the courtyard of Trinity college, lit as it was by June sunlight.

She'd wandered into Trinity seeking the legendary Book of Kells which nuns at her school had always exhorted her to see. Instead she discovered a boy with a scarlet shirt, a dapper moustache, who looked as though he was out of an advertisement for toothpaste. They talked, but talk didn't come to much until Jamesy encountered her later in the summer, she magically transformed into a model, explosive in maroon and purple scarves.

They dated. Unlike Sarah she responded to his approach. They drank wine, lazed by Sandycove pier on striped deck-chairs, she losing her Dublin working-class accent, he losing his élite one. On August 23 they decided to marry. Broached, his parents nearly died, but being Anglo-Irish were accustomed to ogres, gnomes and happenings of a disturbed and illicit nature. So they accepted it. Her family being of simple Dublin working-class stock, the class who had elevated James Larkin as mini-Christ in the early part of the century, now rejoiced that their daughter was marrying into another tribe, the rich. They festooned her properly, admired the petite female with the virtually crimson hair, watched her walk to the altar in a dress made by the bevy of nuns who'd educated her in a concentration camp-type Dublin convent.

52

We were all invited, Sarah, Liam, Christine, me, and we journeyed from the country or from Dublin to attend the wedding in a Dalkey hotel. I had my father's car which I drove from the country and I collected beatified versions of Sarah and Christine that morning, driving them first to a church, then to the reception.

The date of the wedding was September 8. As it was autumn light had left the sky by the time the festivities had reached a zenith. There were the odd in-gathering lights on Dublin Bay, a colour as though in a bad technicolour film on the water and a band of silver on the skyline as though over the skyline there began a different world from ours, out of reach of this country, this insanity, this place where aristocrat and worker could meet in a dazzling reception in a Dalkey hotel.

The Dublin working-class family was mainly assembled on one side and the Anglo-Irish people, gaunt, suspicious, on another, women who looked like lean greyhounds holding glasses of sherry. A priest was drunk among the working-class revellers – the wedding had taken place in a Catholic church – and a young man in a positively luminous white shirt sang, bewitching fat women, 'Love is a many splendoured thing' while one particular fat woman wept. The bride was dressed in green come evening, the groom in white. Film people were there, theatre people, casual by-standers from the newspaper world. The girl, Maria, could be seen on the front of Irish fashion magazines and already she was commissioned for photographs abroad. Jamesy was going to work in the BBC in London as a junior cameraman, giving up his studies.

This was more than a wedding, it was an exile's farewell for them. Jamesy's mother danced with a foreign diplomat and a fat working-class lady fell on the floor. Someone somewhere in the course of the evening was heard to whisper, 'And the fire and the rose are one', and a band played regular Glenn Miller and Benny Goodman numbers, and young and old paraded their bodies, their souls, in their handkerchiefs, in dance.

Jamesy was cool to us, a lost friend, but now he and his wife already formed a spurious off-spring of the show-business world. He was quickly retreating into his father's theatrics.

Jamesy's father sat in a corner, bow-tie open and he reminiscing about Synge and Lady Gregory and Yeats. He claimed to have a tinge of Synge's blood in his family and that would not surprise me, given Jamesy's dashing features.

We danced together, Sarah, Liam, Christine, me. I realized more than ever that Christine was not my requisition, more fated to me as a coincidence. It was like buying one brand of tea because another was not available. In the last days of August I'd visited Dublin, Liam absent, stayed in the flat, met Sarah often, had afternoon tea with her in the Shelbourne. This evening, my fingers tipping her shoulders in a waltz I realized she was my real lover, her curls, her hair, her jewellery like trinkets on a Waterford glass chandelier. I didn't know how to phrase the next section of my life. I knew what it was going to be.

I was going to have an affair with Sarah.

Liam danced with Sarah, athletic boy, blond haired, quiff falling like late summer leaves, eyes intense, shoulders hunched. He was hunched like a young academic, broad shouldered like a military man. He had a black blazer, white shirt, his back in dancing like an instrument in motion. He swayed like a Benny Goodman trombone. I noticed the intensity of his pose, forehead autographed not just by the past but by the future, furrowed a little, the daring of his mother there, her beauty, the day she put on dark glasses in the garden and read a poem by John Clare from a book like a child's missal. I recognized the continuity of these moments that night, that the dead don't die but linger, that Mrs Kenneally was with us, woman in a purple summer dress with polka dots, haunches hunched into a deckchair and she expostulating about Stalin or the river Volga or the local priest's abomination of whiskey and preference for vodka.

I left Christine and stared, stared at the dancing couple as though at the hurt and brilliance of history, knew that moment

54

that these people were destined to be hurt, Liam, Sarah, hurt terribly, that the good always die a multitude of deaths and I was reminded of the words of an artist long ago, a maker of stained glass, who quoted from St Teresa of Avila.

> Not a friend was by his side
> When his cross he did embrace
> And to us came light and grace
> Through our Lord the crucified.

There were gay songs and abandoned songs that night, none more beautiful than a young Dublin girl's rendition, at the close of the party, of 'Ave Maria'. I stumbled to the lavatory afterwards, urinating as I watched myself in a mirror, stumbled out, found Sarah and Liam embracing in a corridor, held them, they holding me, all three of us there, a pagoda of love for these moments until I saw Christine come to a corner, spy us, run away.

Liam made to look for her and I said, 'Don't bother,' and later, Christine nowhere to be found, I drove Sarah home first, then Liam and myself back to the flat, thinking all the time about leaves, the leaves on grey beside Liam's home and the photographs in the men's club of intense First World War men, their ladies and a letter from the war front, framed, from a young man to his sweetheart, recounting the day they'd bought a spiral of balloons at the fair and freed them into the air about the October, sunlit town.

I still went out with Christine that autumn. She'd given up college and was learning to type, having moved out of her aunt's, staying in a flat with girls from the country. We went to films, watched plays, a matter of course, as Sarah and Liam cycled about together or feasted on honey brown cakes in the Monument Café. Dublin that autumn was full of cyclists on daunting metallic bicycles, rain, queer brands of nuns. It was as though there was an invasion of nuns, nuns from Mars, nuns from Saturn. And all the time – in the unrelenting rain – people queued to see Pier Angeli or Robert Donat, technicolour smiles in a city of forfeited jobs, forfeited birthright.

But the times Christine and I encountered Liam and Sarah directly were fewer. They were more a couple, Christine and I playing out the last airs and graces of our romance. Eventually that autumn, I can't remember how or where, maybe over a bleeding ice-cream in the Metropole or over a Bloody Mary in the Shelbourne lounge, the cord snapped with Christine. I abandoned her to the Dublin night.

Then we were a threesome, almost by accident, Sarah, Liam, I. We went places together. No Jamesy, no Christine, just the survivors, unshackled by crowds.

There was the flat, less sex between Sarah and Liam, more conversation, meals, boats going to England and evenings with night growing like a New York jazz musician's version of blue. One returned to a radical simplicity in those weeks. One began again, the complications of sex and crowds less, more an opportunity again to reassess, to weigh up with the mind and the soul, rather than with instant infatuation.

Liam went to see Christine once, an aside. He told me about it. She was living in a flat with other girls from the country. The flat was big and cold, an odd decimated picture of Roy Rogers on the wall. The girls were like dormice and looked at Liam as though he was a Russian count visiting Ahascraugh or Athlone. They'd gone to the pictures, Christine and Liam, sat through *The Naked Jungle*, a middle-aged Dublin urchin playing with himself and the ice-cream woman, a fat lady, eating her own ice-creams. It was late and raining when they returned to Christine's flat so Liam stayed the evening there, sleeping alongside her in a bed as big as a country bed which accommodated old farmers and their wives.

'She looked odd,' Liam said, 'drained. A look in her eyes like life gone from them and a worry there, a pain that hadn't been there before.'

I didn't really want to listen. I harkened to the chorus of cries rising from a rugby pitch or to the sound of storm over the

Irish Sea but not to news of Christine. She was a dead letter, first love, in a literal sense, but really just a person I'd bided my time with, waiting for Sarah.

In a winter of desecration Sarah spoke of those who'd resisted Hitler. Dietrich Bonhoeffer, the Legion of Mary, the few voices of resistance rising above a nation consumed by an orgy of evil. 'There are always those,' she said, 'who light candles of faith,' while macabre Dublin women trailed the streets of Dublin with lighted candles singing 'The Bells of the Angelus', in mindfulness of cardinals, priests and prelates stuck behind the iron curtain of their imaginations. Liam and I strained to catch Sarah's words, boats dipping over the Dublin horizon, lights going out.

We went to a school dance at Sarah's former school, both had turns dancing with Sarah, spoke to an old teacher of Sarah's who told us about the Spanish civil war, a time as head of a convent, leading her community from place to place about an indecisive battlefront.

'There was no clear cause,' the nun said, 'just atrocities. War breeds monsters in all camps.'

Just before Christmas we were invited to Sarah's home for the first time. Her parents were throwing a dinner party and Liam and I, bearing bottles of paraffin-coloured wine wrapped in frail brown paper, journeyed to Rathgar, becoming wet by virtue of rain edging from the nearby mountains.

A fire blazed triumphantly. Old men, old women stood around. As in Liam's home the area over the fireplace was preoccupied by a painting of Aran, women in scarlet, the sea, currachs, men with caps and plaintiveness in their eyes.

We were introduced to a woman, a niece of Sarah's father, shortly to journey to the United Nations to join the first Irish delegation there. A middle-aged priest spoke loudly about the evening light falling in autumn on the Blasket Islands, rabbits racing, marigold beds still ablaze and the Atlantic winter imminent, huge drifts of cloud over the sun. Sarah's father spoke to a painter, seated. Sarah's mother, standing, a raven haired woman, addressed an old lady about the possibility of starting a polio clinic. Ireland's entry into the United Nations was much discussed.

'We now have a place among nations,' a wizened old lawyer said.

But I recognized something in Sarah's father that night, a kind of inarticulate disappointment those moments he just sat and took things in. He was a man, sixty, who'd trailed with English aristocrats wearing buttercup-type flowers in their bonnets to Connemara cottages early in the century to learn Gaelic. A young man he'd accompanied arch socialists and romantics to fight on the streets of Dublin in 1916. A young doctor, he'd quickly risen to the height of his profession, now a surgeon famed among the poor. But he'd seen bridges crash, ignorant men take over and smother a nation in the abuse of privilege, learning and moral code. He'd seen a country worse than it had been before, grinding to a halt, more than anything a kind of speechlessness about the poor. His work brought him close to these people and as such he was respected, someone who gave his genius to women burdened by too many pregnancies, those who hailed from hideous red brick flats bearing wounds, varicose veins, faces varicose and pained with generations of suppression and deprivation.

In the course of the evening a lady sang 'I have seen the lark in the morning' as whiskeys trembled in abeyance, and immediately afterwards Sarah's mother announced that she hoped to set up a polio clinic in the near future.

Guests were shown to the door.

The rain had eased off and as Liam and I left I thought I heard the priest say in Gaelic 'Is spré an rud óige.' 'Youth is a graceful thing.'

Christmas at home was brief that year. We were anxious to get back to Dublin to be with Sarah. Liam left his father, a man ageing quickly, and took an early morning train back to Dublin with me.

Another party was held in Sarah's house to mark the New

Year. We were invited, formally Sarah's friends. We arrived in sleeveless white jerseys, banded by blue, ties thick, well groomed young men. It was more crowded than the last time, searching faces in evidence everywhere, the Aran islands, the women in scarlet all but blocked out. Conversation was more inspired by drink than by intellectual awareness. The ageing social princesses of Dublin pranced about. Surgeons issued disclosures about their existences, 'Well I'm not really a man of genius, merely a doctor,' while painters drummed up sympathy for the arts, 'No one's buying our paintings except Tory M.P.s in Britain.'

A gentle civil servant who'd had his book banned by the government started to cry in the course of the evening while Sarah's father argued with a man who accused him of betrayal, betrayal of the ideals of the men of 1916, allying himself with the Free State government. 'I'm a worker,' Sarah's father said, 'a doctor.'

'Joining the queue to Arbour Hill every year. Honouring the dead. Betraying the living.'

'I have no part in this government. I heal casualties. I tend to those in need.'

'And you indulge in this charade, each year the tricolour, the wreaths, the brass band, the military salute.'

'I honour the dead.'

The man was referring to the yearly commemoration of the 1916 martyrs, a pagan feast of women in black, wreaths, and tricolours with an extra dash of gold.

Sarah had taken part in these as a child, a doll in black.

The music ceased as the journalists, the writers, the artists watched, delighted with the fracas, and Sarah's father calmly, nobly left his enemy, walked with the stride of a Prussian officer to the piano and commenced Mendelssohn's 'Waltz of the Clowns' at which point the party began again, the smoke signals of conversation rose again, the priests spoke about Gaelic Elysium and the poets gabbled to one another about acquaintances long dead who had never walked the length of Stephen's

Green without stopping in conversation over a bunch of hydrangeas, discussing art, politics or bygone prelates.

The new year sent bouquets of frost, frost over Dublin, frost on the mountains, frost on the streets.

Sarah, an emissary, went to the Catholic workers' association, to Trade Union meetings. She wanted to know all, to figure out the hieroglyphics of what it was like to be poor.

Her father worked harder, washing his hands in the blood of Dublin working women, in their wounds, delivering their babies, tending to their gynaecological deficiencies, returning home, albeit rarely, to a wife who had her hair the colour of Connemara crows, and to a daughter who was adept at preparing beautiful meals, nursing a cooking chicken until it emerged shimmering with gold, to be devoured to the sound of Bach and the fizz of French wine.

I knew by Liam that he felt he was intruding, that Sarah had become closer to her family. One had to handle her more gently, a shell by the sea, a fragment of ancient parchment. One had to wait one's due. Liam became impatient, thrown back in my company. He began buying a lot of wine, reading Victorian pornography, lying in lewd poses in bed.

One evening I found him asleep – naked – on an eiderdown and covered him. A fog-horn sounded.

I'd just dated a girl called Laura, bringing her to the pictures. My nostrils were full of the rose lining of Dublin cinema seats and the smoky, cigarette fumed air. I went to the window. For the first time, looking at the sea, I perceived direction, all the possible paths people could take, the infinite aura of self-made choice. I sat down, read the *Irish Times*, saw that a cardinal had been impeached by an East European government and that an American housewife had been accused of storing *Das Kapital* under her bed.

The three of us travelled a bit, to cinema, opera, play and to little places in Wicklow. Liam, Sarah slept together on Saturday nights. With Sarah moods changed quick as the drift of cigarette smoke in open cafés. After withdrawal she was again the whore of Babylon, sheathed in damson or black. Her lover made her moan in the night, made her grieve. I often felt an unutterable desire to touch them, these lovers, before they evaporated, and one night, the three of us having gone to see *Carmen Jones*, afterwards having drunk liquorice wine, I waited until Liam and Sarah lay soundless in their big bed, then left my own, politely putting back the sheets, climbed in beside them, my underpants slipping down, lay there knowing them to be awake, receiving my presence, conniving with it, though never mentioning it in the weeks afterwards when spring returned bearing men with bowler hats in Stephen's Green and a new silence emerged, the silence of knowledge never taught, learnt.

Sarah in a vanilla dress, handbag in her fist, spoke to old men about the weather, roused flagging interest in nuns in St Teresa of Avila, caused unbeknownst arousal of sex in young clerics. She drifted, a cataclysm in people's lives, her beauty that of a Botticelli Venus, her clothes were always considered, informed with a private passion for things beautiful but not too beautiful, exact.

It was 23 March 1956 when I returned from an outing with the mountaineering club, found Liam and Sarah in bed together, this time without any qualms undressed to my underpants, got in beside them, covered myself and some time in the night woke to find Liam and Sarah making love.

That done I touched Sarah, her nipples, her furze of pubic hair. I pulled towards her, roused into her, making love to someone who after all was just a nineteen or twenty-year-old girl.

The postage stamps that time in Ireland were terrible, were tasteless, the weather generally disgusting, the kind of art being produced unimaginative, the artistic elders arthritic, the fine books banned, the Fitzgeralds, the Hemingways. There was nothing, but nothing, to recommend this retarded island and yet we, Liam Kenneally, Sarah Thompson, me Sean McMahon, danced a fine dance, wore bow-ties, cravats to advertise a vice. It should have been Paris, should have been Berlin but being Dublin the experience was none the worse for that, just that the ensemble of lavatories smelled worse, and the sky implored just too much rain.

Let me tell you about Liam's body, fine, supple like hurling sticks. Sarah's was neat as new roses and mine, mine was the conventional one, the one that exercised calm, control. But we made love often, Sarah, Liam, I. We bought bottles of wine which had strayed from Algeria. We got to know one another, a Biblical phrase, body and soul.

One never realizes later how long these affairs last, days, months, years. There's no real chronology, a few hours maybe, but later those hours prevail like years, a time untouched until Greek gods send telegrams and an island, peaceful, baleful, in the Aegean is disturbed by death.

Our telegram arrived on a wet, almost wintry day when the cherry blossom had emerged in Earlsfort Terrace. A young cleric approached me, a bedraggled late arrival from bed, to tell me, 'You know your friend Sarah Thompson. Her father's just died.'

It couldn't have been more appropriate. I'd just been reading the story of Telemachus in bed.

I stopped. My head bowed. Somehow life had stumbled on its own truth.

She held daffodils at the funeral. She was dressed in black alongside her mother. Her curls fused from beneath a cap, a bonnet of gold. A priest read an oration. Wizened Dublin charwomen held back tears against the rain.

The funeral over words were few. There was a reception in Sarah's home, salad, wine, as though this was not the aftermath of a funeral but the celebration of art, life, conquest. Sarah, unprompted, reached for the piano keys and played, silence drifting and heads turning, Mendelssohn's 'Waltz of the Clowns'.

The bereaved daughter visited Liam's home after Easter. She stayed in a big room looking towards the convent, the tiny sanctuaries for birds and nuns, the episcopal river. The wail of orphans called from her bed, little boys and girls still without parents, the air rebounding with their pain.

It was extraordinary to watch her, strolling with Liam's father down the passage leading to the garden, lamb-white cardigan over her shoulders. They got on extremely well, discussing obscure works by Tolstoy or William Morris's ideas of social reform. One was struck not just by her beauty but by the heritage of this moment. Sarah Thompson bore a remarkable resemblance to her forbear, Elizabeth Kenneally. She was unaware of similarities, a fragment of bone structure, a whiff of blonde on pale Nordic skin, the breadth of her shoulders, her inquisitive hunch.

Somehow Liam and I were left out of the picture. It was an episode between Dr Kenneally and Sarah, languorous conversations and an eye always in the garden to the weather, the sudden squalls that blew in from heather bog or distant ocean.

Summer term a curious thing occurred. This affair which flourished beneath red and white striped awning for Liam and Sarah suddenly shifted emphasis. I was now intermingled in their moments together and suddenly out of this confusion emerged an unexpected pattern. Sarah Thompson more often than not clung to me for friendship, conversation. Drinking ice-cool orange in the Shelbourne lounge or slender glasses of iced coffee in Bewley's it was me she touched, my hand she chose recognizing somewhere inside her, I think, that in the aftermath of death she and Liam were too close, both having intuited death.

Of the two of us I was the simpler, the less confused, the one more likely to lead a normal unruffled life. So Sarah chose me, my evenness, the journey of my experiments which any day could glide into normality and the social acceptability wrought by a desire for the untwisted truth, the commonplace. Liam sensed this. The ease of our camaraderie, our laughter.

One afternoon he returned to find us in bed together and that was it. Some essential privacy eroded, the boy with the blond hair by the lace curtains horrified, frozen into a new realization that abysmal love affairs don't necessarily last, that beautiful relationships don't necessarily continue, rising and shooting forth like spring leeks.

On a day in mid-May Liam hopped on a train for the North, visiting distant relatives who lived on the extreme north coast of Antrim. When he returned, his birthday buried in those days, he informed me and Sarah about them, sitting in a morning tea-house as though nothing had happened, nothing had come between us.

His relatives were Protestants, living in a bungalow by the ocean, a husband, wife, two daughters. The wife dressed in semi-Victorian clothes and had been instrumental in founding a free school in Scotland. Their garden held a bounty of fruit and vegetables. Their house accommodated lost masterpieces by Irish mystic painters and two very Trojan Irish wolfhounds manned the ocean against invaders. Liam's uncle had a beard more like whiskers and wore high stockings, striped blue and white and a pair of pantaloons. He owned a factory in Belfast and talked with Liam about bygone collectors of folklore or botanists famed or infamous for some moral peculiarity in their character. The daughters were both painters, running to and fro to Paris.

But of one thing Liam's uncle was firm, the foolhardiness of the Irish Free State. 'A cabal of fools.' 1916 he said was an idiot's outing, a party game for entrepreneurs, do-gooders, academic deviants and political hysterics. Suddenly on a beach in north Antrim Liam found himself defending the revolutionaries of 1916.

Men of honour, he said. Noble men. Men who aspired to the political unity of a country. Men who changed history. Men who founded a new state, as yet uncertain of itself, but born of such nobility of character and statement bound some day for great things. His uncle had shrugged. Under no circumstances would he ever surrender his Unionist kingdom to the Southern State. Freedom was priceless he said. Freedom from bigotry. Freedom from mind-boggling obscurantism.

The wind blew in, became harsh on their faces. The con-

64

versation ceased. They retired to cups of hot cocoa and a view of the sea, turbulent under a May storm.

Somehow the potential argument, confusion between Sarah, me and Liam disappeared in the advent of final examinations. One drank much orange. One lazed in the garden.

Sarah's mother invited us both to dinner one evening and we sat in the kitchen, eating on an old wooden table, without the sun secretive and deep with evening. Sarah's mother had cooked a dish of red cabbage and chicken and we ate peaceably. 'You have two boy-friends,' Sarah's mother said over the meal to Sarah, 'what an exciting time you must have.'

We drank tea in the parlour and the lady spoke of her polio clinic, her hopes for it, for raising money, for dedicating it to her husband's memory. There was a frail woodpecker-like quality about the woman, her face in evening sunlight looked even more sharpened and resolute.

'Basically,' she said, 'I wish to continue with what Gerard was doing, building a sanctuary one way or the other for the defenceless.'

Liam spoke a little about Galway, his home, the river, the convent, the orphans, his mother, the dead Russian woman with the face fine as red sandstone along the river Volga and the body firm as a river going vessel. I spoke about my parents; my father, a well-known lawyer, of Dublin origin, my mother of a well-to-do Westmeath farming household.

Origins waved aside we discussed art and Mrs Thompson brought us to her bedroom and fetched a painting from under her bed, a newly acquired one by Jack B. Yeats. *The Arab bids farewell to his Steed*, a horse, white, dying in the fold of his maroon clothed Arab.

I went to the window and looked out at the emerald lawns of Dublin, held for a moment before being relinquished into darkness. It was our last summer at college, perhaps our last summer in Dublin. I waited for that final moment of darkness and accompanied Sarah, her mother, Liam down to the parlour again for tea before parting.

After the final examinations due to be held in September Liam and Sarah planned to go away together. It was as though they'd renegued on all confusion in their relationship and wanted to prove they were one. Examinations over, a huge tiredness lifted, they left the North Wall in Dublin, heading south.

I went home for some weeks, watched the ebullience of harvest by the river, connived in little tea-parties in the back gardens of limestone houses, lingered gently over what to do next, then journeyed back to Dublin to become an apprentice in a solicitor's office.

Autumn gave way to winter, evidence in the soft air of cold, of tormented spray. A cold wind blew Baggot Street to nudity.

Copies of the *Irish Times* accumulated on a solicitor's desk. News of hurlers, prelates, American politicians. Then one day Hungary was invaded and Sarah returned.

Her body burned into mine weeks of November. Fear, pain in her limbs, breasts. She looked older, harrowed. She'd lost weight, her eyes big like an East European orphan. But she didn't speak of her weeks with Liam until much, much later, some aspect of Hell caught sight of.

They'd gone south to the exotic, untravelled places of the South of France. Cannes, Nice, Monte Carlo. The last of summer penetrated Antibes and old women, seated on benches in Monte Carlo gazed south. The ghost of Camus was felt in Monte Carlo, a game of baccarat intuited, the weather changing, autumn arriving, a definitive grey. The couple traversed a border to Italy; on a train to Verona a drunk offered them wine. 'Romeo e Giulietta,' he remarked.

Il Trovatore was sung in Verona, a soprano's voice echoing over a darkening Roman city.

In Venice they knew it was over; they encountered a wall, nowhere further to go, row after row making them both violent in different ways, she sulking, introverted, he smashing her face with his hand one morning. That was it.

She turned back, a waif on the train consuming bread, encountering a Hungarian girl wearing a flame-like scarf who informed her of the rising in Budapest.

Where was Liam? One didn't know.

The weather became unexpectedly bad in Dublin, the Dublin mountains breathing foul gusts of rain like a dragon.

Women who had previously been contained were inspired by madness, running around the streets of Dublin shouting about the Pope, captive cardinals, the Hungarian rising. Banners bearing ikons of cardinals enthralled the skyline and women with faces without eyes marched the streets, the city exploding into one unified candle flame. A Hungarian communist living in a Dublin block of flats was besieged and generally an ancient fear ambled in the streets of Dublin, fear of a vacuum always present in Irish life, rarely acknowledged.

Sarah became pale and thin like a child in a war. Eventually even my Trojan efforts could not appease her and she wept a lot, broke down crying in an odd trail of places like the Monument Café, the Shelbourne lounge. She took to wearing dour clothes, browns, near blacks, a widow's weeds. The only colour in her disenchanted appearance was an odd scarf of white, with naive emerald dots. Sometimes she looked aged, sometimes a twelve-year-old orphan. I knew her to be travelling to a frontier. There was no name for this frontier. No one had travelled to it before.

The women of Dublin looked mournful as the statues of the Madonna in dark suburban churches.

I wanted to reach to Sarah, to call her back. I knew Liam would have a power over her if he'd been here. But he was nowhere in sight.

Prostitutes dangled by the canal. Politicians' widows presented flowers to nuns. Even the mannequins in Brown Thomas' window mourned.

Sarah began going to mass, repentant. Visiting the poor, giving the alms of her beauty, giving advice. She took to social work, social investigation. She visited the over-burdened women her father had tended and on December 10 told me she was

67

going to be a nun in a stiff, self-punishing order who administered to the poor. I knew she'd flown from us in insanity. Outside Bewley's Oriental Café in Grafton Street there was little or nothing I could say.

She told me that her father's death had affected her deeper than anyone had known, that the idea of death had left a crater in her life as empty as the moon, that the only way she could cope with it was to devote her life to the transcendance of death and to work which would regain for her the kingdom of the spirit, the area she'd known tending with her father the bee-hives in the back garden or the infinite area of marigolds in the front garden, a patch-work of oranges and golds which infused the mind and set the spirit aflame.

She was holding a handbag. Her coat was long and brown. She told me gently she did not wish to see me again. Her mother she said knew of her decision. She would go north to Drogheda, dress in a habit white as skulls, kneel before crimson Christs like the poor of Dublin did, eventually journey abroad to Africa, redressing the ignorance of the Western world which abandoned huge areas of the universe to starvation. 'I want,' she said, 'to be. I haven't been since Daddy died. I want to continue doing, trying to make the world an easier place to live in.'

Her choosing of orthodox Catholicism to do this was her perversity. She subjected herself to cannibalistic rites to prove the humility of her intentions. There was something almost pantomimic about her outside Bewley's. One would almost have demanded a halo for her.

December 11 a letter came from Liam.

113 Heath Road,
London S.W.8.
26 November 1956

Dear Sean,

How are you? I'm living here in London, working for British Rail. I found a room in Battersea. It's lovely cycling to work in the morning. I bought a bicycle for 2/6. The weather's cold. I pass by Cheyne Walk in the mornings where George Eliot and Swinburne lived. The foreman thinks I'm in the I.R.A. but I say I'm half-Russian. Then he tells me I'm a Red.

London is full of storm clouds but there are moments when the sun comes out.

How's Sarah?

Tell her I was asking for her.

Tell her I'll see her soon, that I have a gift for her, a locket with a genuine Russian ikon inside. It's beautiful. Gold and black. I'm filled with grief here. But then there's always Ireland.

> Love and farewell,
> Liam.

By some crux the letter came too late. Sarah had already journeyed to a macabre destiny.

I met him off the boat at Christmas, Liam changed, hollowed like a young soldier.

He went to see Sarah. I told him not to. It was devastating for him, a young woman in white under a picture of St Anthony surrounded by writhing demons. She looked at him, eyes like patient rubies but a farawayness about them. She didn't see him, didn't acknowledge him. Sarah was in the grip of her own demons. I told Liam that it was guilt, her father's guilt over a broken statelet, passed on to her, that she was making amends for the failure of the 1916 revolution, but Liam had gone beyond another frontier, the frontier of comfort.

He went home, stayed with his father, found a room in Galway city, giving tuition in English, and I lived in a big apartment in Donnybrook with a young Roscommon man. This man was a teacher, a national school teacher, one always talking about the Fenians, the Famine, French writers who had died in the First World War and British poets. His name was Michael and I rarely saw him. I was dating a young girl called Laura. We fed ourselves on Hollywood movies and pop-corn.

She was from the countryside near my home, a member of parliament's daughter. In Dublin she studied domestic science. The Dublin skyline blurred for us, was wicked for us, but not excessive. It told the truth about two young people up from the country, more than likely destined to return to it. About this time Christine reappeared. I met her in a pub one evening. A famous literary pub with high ceilings and rounded stained glass. She was with a poet, scarf on her head, cigarette in her mouth, sluttish, sullen, but her face still the arabesque of a clown's, full of wrinkles and smiles.

I was with Laura. I sat with Christine, spoke to her. It emerged she lived with her poet. She washed floors. He wrote. He was from a big town in Kerry. His accent was an offspring of that county and his prose larded with poetry and extravagant quotations from Gaelic poets who'd served on ships in the eighteenth century. He came from a large merchant family, now had designs on Olympus. Around were numerous other would-be poets, their women, women just, men just, glinting bachelors, barmen with an eye for beauty. A middle-aged lady with hair red as Maureen O'Hara's sang 'Carrickfergus'. Tears came to many faces. A German student was enthralled.

But beneath the cloak of romanticism Christine just turned to me and whispered 'Where is he?' meaning Liam and I knew by her eyes that it was Liam she still hated, not me.

She lived in a rough dungeon of a place off Grafton Street. She lived next to a church. As of old she never said prayers but watched Dublin's poor ebb and flow from mass. Christine Canavan had cultivated a bitterness all this time. I could see it in her, a pain as deep as rejection, a sliver as of desert sand in a light breeze. She was still hurt by Liam, hurt by him as of the night she discovered he and Sarah were lovers. I at least had succumbed to her, been her lover in my twisted retrograde Catholic way.

As there was a renewed I.R.A. campaign in the North, bridges blown up, radio stations, electricity installations, the literary population of Dublin pledged themselves to support the victimized Catholics and Christine's lover went off North one day with a gun, a bunch of ragged winter roses and a bottle of cheap wine. He was found some days later drunk in a Dundalk bar.

Christine entertained the literary populace of Dublin in her flat, the drunks, the fallen women. I touched on her life, me and Laura going to see her once or twice with a carton of Guinness. I visited her as though revisiting a hesitant point in my life. There was less I needed to know about Liam, Sarah, Christine. I was free of past, had a tranquil girlfriend, played rugby on filthy pitches.

But occasionally, just occasionally a face haunted, Sarah's in the wet of Grafton Street, a virgin again, disconsolate in the never yielding, forever blackening Dublin rain. I didn't wish to tell Laura about this part of my life. I went to Christine's parties as though observing a ghost in motion, intrigued that I should once have been other than I was now, a young man on his proper course.

In March Liam came up from Galway to stay with me. There was evidence of initial blossoms. March breezes rushing to and fro and everywhere the ripple, the return of life.

A famed American poet visited town and one day threatened to throw himself out of the Gresham Hotel, standing on an upper window, a delighted crowd rallying below, Christine in a brown coat among their number.

I was going somewhat between Christine and Liam. Christine's lover ran naked down a Dublin back street one night, was caught, brought to court, fined despite protest from illustrious relatives.

'The sow who eats her own farrow,' he was heard to whisper. He and Christine were planning on leaving. Up and going to Paris. A tricolour raged against a souring St Patrick's Day sky. Mother Ireland was waving farewell to her vigilant young.

Bombs exploded in the North, Brookborough Bridge was blown up and a ripe young body returned, that of Sean South, killed in action. For weeks now the population of Southern

71

Ireland did not know what to make of renewed war but with the possibility of a hero they turned out in droves, Franciscan friars like medieval devils blessing the coffin and a nation singing 'A Nation once again' and 'Faith of our Fathers' until suddenly the people of the South tired of this folly and forgot it.

A noted botanist threw a party in Killiney one night. Liam and I were invited. It was May. We got an 8 bus there, walking from Dalkey. Inside the door crowded with eager Dublin faces I perceived Christine. Now a curious thing had happened in those weeks. Liam had become friendly with a girl, a confidante of Christine's. Somehow they'd had amorous contact. It hadn't worked – the memory of Sarah was too deep in Liam – and in the course of the party, Christine drinking like a goldfish became irately drunk, pushed her way to the front of the crowd and began shouting in Liam's face.

'You're incapable, incapable of making love.' There were a few derisive sniggers, silence, Christine evaporated into the crowd and again talk was about a show by Tennessee Williams, wherein the actors were being brought to court for displaying a contraceptive on stage.

'He was led like a sheep to be slaughtered and like a lamb that's dumb before the shearer he does not open his mouth. He has been humiliated and has no redress. Who will be able to speak of his posterity? For he is cut off from the world of living men.' His figure became more wasted, his eyes swallowed in pain. Nothing reached him, the Tennessee Williams' show, news that my flat-mate had been arrested while on a raid to the North – he'd been a member of the I.R.A. all this time. These signs were wasted on him.

Christine up and went to Paris. The last I saw of her was on O'Connell Bridge, scarlet scarf blowing against the lowly skyline known to poet and painter.

He saw me dating a lovely country girl, knew that no matter what happened I'd be O.K. He applied for many jobs, many scholarships. In June he received news that he'd been accepted on scholarship to an American university to do a thesis on the

American poet Hart Crane. Though it was summer it might have been winter, a new agè had come, laughter scarcer, broad brimmed hats fewer and pleasure in the hands of glutton, not artist.

On August 23 Liam's father drove to Dublin. He entertained Liam and me in the Shelbourne lounge. We had lemonade. Then we commenced on afternoon tea. Liam had run Sarah's house the previous evening. Sarah's mother answered. Sarah had finished her period as a postulant and had entered the novitiate.

I could feel the edge in Liam's voice, the greyness, the stammer swift as a woodbine cigarette in the hands of a nervous cleric.

Women shot their wares of marigolds against Nelson's pillar. A Pier Angeli feature was advertised at the Ambassador. A brand of cigarettes was flaunted over the entrance to the slum area of Sean McDermott Street.

I knew he was thinking of Sarah, of Walt Whitman, of the boat going to England from Dun Laoghaire pier. I knew by the look on his face.

We arrived at the airport.

'You haven't been home all summer,' Liam's father said.

Liam's face looked curiously lamb-like against the sultry August sky. His eyes for one moment turned blue, the blue the sky should have been. I wanted to touch his lips, his body, to greet him like one cavalier to another. That was no longer possible. Liam's father was mumbling about modern American poets – a senior Belgian diplomat was shown through the airport – and an Aer Lingus plane took off for London, its nose seeking the sky like a watchful terrier.

'You'll be home soon.' Words dashed, stubbed against the sky. A scream was rising within me worse than planes taking off.

'It's lovely at home,' Liam's father said. He talked of the river. I'd had a nightmare the river had run dry. He talked of the garden forever blooming and eventually he mentioned Elizabeth Kenneally.

'She'll be praying for you,' Liam's father said like a remorseful Catholic.

I enumerated these things in my mind, orphans, peas, leeks, an oak tree, striped deck-chairs, a Russian woman, gone mad with the grief of living, Irish Catholicism, missals, and somewhere stuck in that experience the faces of Christine, unrepentant, Sarah, another Irish woman somehow unable to contain her purity.

The moments dragged like years of history. Nuns were packed off to Rome. Sarah would be going to Africa on one of those planes. Liam's father droned about the Galway races. Horses raced in my mind, coming into the final post.

I held out a hand.

'Liam, goodbye,' I said.

He looked at me. His eyes were blue, blue of the sea, blue of the Californian sky to which he was heading, blue of a country far, far happier than the one he was leaving. He was like a dying person who wanted to say something but couldn't. I watched him walk away. I wanted to cry but I didn't. I knew my tears would not help.

I turned away. Though I would not be at the airport when Sarah would be going I said goodbye to Sarah then too, and to Christine. 'They'll be selling peaches now,' Liam's father said, 'at the Leopardstown races.' And I looked at him and thought him a man gone mad. A plane screamed into time and history.

I had a secret that I shared with no one. When my flat-mate was arrested after his mysterious disappearance the flat was raided. Little of interest was discovered – a novel by Paul Claudel, Davitt's account of his prison days in Tasmania – but on a summer's morning spring-cleaning I found a gun under the floorboards. A treasure. I kept it there. For me it spoke of that young man's daring and the silent grief of Northern Irish Catholics. I held on to it, often lifting the floorboards to admire it. In one moment if I fired it I would shatter a heritage into fragments. I returned home that evening. My girlfriend had ceased her studies and was back in Galway. Huge tractors were digging craters outside, preparing the way for a massive new hospital.

I opened the floorboards, took out the gun. I stood before a mirror, gun to my head, recalling Camus' ultimate dictum on suicide, knew there were two choices, to live or to die, understood the dictatorship of the mundane, knew looking at a mirror which refracted tractors tunnelling through clay that I was not the suicidal type.

I put the gun down.

Yes, that young man I'd been sharing my flat with had been funny even if I hadn't noticed.

I reread a letter from my father, asking me to return home and be his assistant. For weeks I'd brooded on the letter. Now I jotted a reply. Yes, I would go home.

I lingered in Dublin some weeks.

Lace was blown from hats in front of ladies' faces. Autumn scoured Marlborough Road. Someone whistled a tune by the Irish poet Patrick Kavanagh that haunts memory like a child's golden coin.

On Raglan Road on an autumn day I met her first and knew
That her dark hair would weave a snare that I might one day
    rue;
I saw the danger, yet I walked along the enchanted way,
And I said let grief be a fallen leaf at the dawning of the day.

On an October day I left Dublin, city of churches, rife with bicycles, young priests and doldrum waitresses, locking the door of a room that held a gun and a lucid picture of Albert Camus and went home.

Book Three

DRIVING TO DERRY on a May evening in 1972 there was much to think about. Sun penetrated the windscreen; sun urged into a ruby over Sligo Bay, distilling the grave of Queen Maeve on Knocknarea into an aura of magic. I was going to meet Liam. The sun eventually planted itself on the sea. Sligo Bay was lost and Donegal took over, inlets, strips of sand, a monumental Gothic castle on the sea. The road wound north through the night. I passed tinker encampments and ridiculously sprawling towns. In Ballyshannon I slept for the night near an alarm clock. Tomorrow I would confront Liam for the first time in fifteen years.

I didn't sleep too well that night. The room was foreign to me, white sheets, narrow windows, antique clocks, chairs, each with a voice, a character.

I sat up, smoked. Gradually the night eased about me, ghosts disappeared, a banshee was recalled to the distant bogs and the inveigling mountains of Donegal and I, Sean McMahon, thirty-seven by the calendar, married with three children, a revered solicitor and public man slept, some Atlantic breeze winnowing through the window-pane and plucking at my hair. Why are there moments when one is called upon to give account of one-self, to reckon with ancient forces one has been seeking to hide or bury in remote places, where no hands will touch, albeit the fingers of a curious child.

I was a father now. I had grown children. Why this detour into the past? There were questions I couldn't answer but I had to obey. The night fell softly on my head and again for a few hours images flung into my life like handballs. I was re-living moments, spruce as new daffodils, tall and healthy as twelve-year-old boys.

The first thing I want to say about those fifteen years — and I want to tell you a lot about them — was that Elizabeth Ken-neally never left us. A woman who contained herself in my years at college walked again, a Lazarus in the years that gave birth to my children. I suppose it was the way that I handled her ghost that allowed her so much freedom but that being so, I'll go on piecing together a time that was almost wasted but wasn't by virtue of Laura, my wife, and my children, Patrick, Annabelle and Jason in that order.

The first time I intuited her was in Avila, spring 1958. I went there with my mother on a pilgrimage. We took a bus. The little convent of St Teresa inspired my mother, a woman of the country, given airs and graces all her life, to pray, a few moments on a pew, recollecting a life of golf and of bridge, a moment of excellence as all these things, the herbs and scents and golf-course earth of bourgeois Ireland rose in defiant prayer to God. I was touched by something else. I'd accompanied my mother much to the chagrin of my girlfriend. But now, caught unawares in a white-washed cell, I was reminded of the artist friend of Mrs Kenneally, a plucky lady in black who defied a bishop once and confessed to an admiration of St Teresa, priestess of the female psyche.

'They shall not deal in silver or in gold.' Teresa of Avila's admonition was a phrasing of what the maker of stained glass had done, what Mrs Kenneally had done by her breakdown, what Sarah had done by joining the nuns and what Liam was doing in California, one of these sepulchral people who disdained ordinary human intercourse to attain some other order of being, more private one, helped by an astonishment with growing things, with the winds and the trees and the turf of this universe.

I'd heard from Liam a few times the previous winter. I imagined him, a young man crossing the grass of Berkeley, a knitted scarf transcending his neck and books beneath his arm, books the colour of egg yolks with faces of grave authors on them, while always lights lit the skyline, lonely, semi-blue American lights.

I held on to his letters for a long time. Then one day by virtue of some travesty they were burnt. I always blamed Laura

80

for that. I never forgave her for it though it was possibly some-
one else who did it. Yet in Avila spring 1958, the jukebox play-
ing Chuck Berry and American girls sitting in cheap bars, I was
with Liam, one hundred per cent, with the spirit of his letters,
a bouquet of words thrown across time.

1005 Ashby,
Berkeley,
22 November 1957

Dear Sean,

How are you? The weather's lovely here. Autumn but the
sky still clear and blue. I live in a little apartment on Ashby.
A room. Photographs of James Joyce looking needled with
frail spectacles, Yeats, the Russian poets Pasternak, Maya-
kovsky. A woman of iron. Anna Akmatova. The room stinks
of dwarf dahlias. I moved in here after staying with an uncle
in San Jose. It's good Sean, good. Wonderful the clear skies,
the clear mornings. One can feel the sea. It's as though I
missed the sea from my life for a very long time. I haven't
met anyone yet. To stroll here, across campus, is to under-
stand something dangerous and lovely, the past. No one
touches me. I can feel the past without any obstacles, touch
your face, Sarah's.

Sometimes I can feel it, a shot; Dublin, the endless days
of rain and the avenues reflecting rain, the nuns and the
varicose veins. I pick out a student, his pimples. I am wakeful
to the shadows of rain. Then it goes.

I am again here.

Yesterday, Sean, I went into San Francisco. In a café in
North Beach I encountered two bearded poets who'd visited
the Aran islands. They gave me their address.

Sometimes it's wonderful to be here. A bridge separates
Berkeley from San Francisco, a frail fine pointed bridge, con-
sumed at night by light and by activity. I often look out my
window at that bridge. There's music here at night, a strange
new music. Songs about highways and runaway teenagers.

If you're feeling sad you get an enormous milkshake bedecked with roses of strawberry juice. Sean, do you think it was all madness, Dublin and all that?

I often see Sarah's face crying in the rain though I don't know if it's her tears or just the rain, splashing down.

I think of you often and wonder about you, there in Ireland. It seems far away now. They tell me the whales are hooting now in the far north and one day I will up and listen to them call. I wish you well Sean.

Send me any copies of the *Irish Times* you can, especially if there are reviews of books by Irish writers.

I'm going to Thanksgiving dinner this week. A professor married to an Irishwoman invited me. Take care of yourself.

Liam.

P.S. Give my love to Daddy.

10 December 1957

Dear Sean,

Went to Thanksgiving dinner. It was great. The Irishwoman turned out to be from Galway. She spoke with a rich Galway accent and the table was marked by festival, turkey, cranberry sauce, sweet potatoes bedecked by marshmallow. Three candles lighting, she addressed me about family, family connections.

I said I had a mother born and raised in Moscow and she said she'd heard of this woman; what a tragedy her death had been.

My mother is famous I suppose; I don't feel very Russian here. I feel totally Irish, as though my roots shoot back to the bards and the cavaliers, the native Irish aristocrats, those who dealt in wine before Cromwell came.

I want to address a huge question to you. Do you believe in time? Last night I looked at the sea and disbelieved in it. I was standing in eternity.

Love,
Liam.

New Year a belated Christmas card had arrived. It bore a Venetian nativity scene, greetings to me and my family.

In February before I left for Avila I got a letter speaking of a trip he'd made south, he'd seen Big Sur, the activity of the ocean and people building newly, a new class of gypsy bearing driftwood from the sea and constructing cabins.

When I returned from Avila it was my turn to write. I wrote about Laura, about the winter, rugby sessions, rain, the geese flying over the river, the tobacco coloured marshland. I told him about Avila, when I went there. I wrote how I thought of his mother in a white cell, the Russian woman with the golden hair and sometimes the unmatching earrings. Then I tore up that letter. It was not appropriate. He had known too much grief without being constantly reminded of that grief, even at a distance of six thousand miles. So instead I wrote about the spring, the journey to Spain, the Spanish gypsies, the wine bars, the white squares, the dissolute Spaniards, my mother's prayers, and the night when donkeys brayed and edifying breezes blew in from Castile.

When both my parents were killed in a head-on collision on the Dublin road that June I wrote too – for comfort. The letter must have been late arriving for I did not receive comfort until September when I wed – and then it was too late.

My parents' death had come when it was least expected, a time of dining in Laura's home, feasting by an oak table, being ministered with country bread, liquid country butter, castles of scones, ramparts of rock buns. Her home was thirteen miles from town, a country house with a black door, a golden knocker, larch trees on either side. Her father usually spent his time in the Dail in Dublin, arguing about the price of cattle or the heads of small farmers. Laura and I were the beatified couple, the couple who most swooned to people's attention by virtue of our compatibility, our acceptable good looks, my job, Laura's father. There seemed to be a defined road in front of us, a road that knew no holes until my parents were killed and townspeople gathered in my home on a mist darkened June evening, expressing their grief, ladies' hats sponged into wetness.

Laura fetched a bottle of Beaujolais that night and the young woman I thought to be a simple country girl opened a bottle of wine and dark hair pulled back on strong buttermilk features said, 'Death is close to festivity. The gods of mirth are forever regarding the gods of death,' surprising me into a new and unique awareness of the girl I'd brought to the pictures and whom I'd mistaken for a simple-minded country coquette.

Over the summer we sailed, swam, ate in the succour of Laura's home, the larch trees buzzing with flies. Often my eyes lingered on Laura's fingers holding a tea-cup printed with blue stripes or a ring on her finger, silver. She had grace, her hair tied back in a ponytail, her features eager, protruding.

I knew death to be reneguing in those summer breezes, I knew doors to be closing on Dublin. I realized inwardly I was beginning again and on no account did I desire to be dragged back to Dublin, to doors leading to certain lounges like the doors of confessionals.

We married in September in a gregarious social wedding. Laura was bedecked in white, white flourishing from her like a bed of begonias. We were photographed against the limp trees of the prom. Her father was bedazzled with smiles. Huge contingents of relatives gathered, uncles, aunts flown back from the States, heavy emerald in evidence in hats and coats.

I wished Liam had been there, but all there was was a card from him, showing a log cabin and redwood trees, from some place in northern California. I realized as the cameras flashed that there was something of his knowingness, his austerity on my face – Liam attended by proxy. He, the elegant young man brimfull of ideas, haunted my features. The card from Liam contained condolence for the fate of my parents, good wishes for my future with Laura, whichever I wished to choose from. I chose neither. His message was too curt, too far away, too oblique and though I replied I didn't hear from him again for fifteen years, nothing, neither wind, ocean or war prevailed upon him to contact me.

The reception for my wedding took place in the local hotel, a floor crowded with antiquated couples waltzing and young secretaries, Laura's comrades from a boarding-school, crowded about her, cheeks red as saffron roses. Laura was the centre of august attention, the first of her class-mates to wed, the most attractive of them, today more matriarch than queen, elegant, watchful, firm.

An orchestra that was falling apart played dilapidated tunes like 'Galway Bay' or 'Bless this House'. Despite the rural background of Laura's relatives there was a near-elegance in the dress, slate greys, Connemara greens, a dullness yet a pride and no face without its distinctive smile. As couples waltzed and Laura betrayed her virtue to a host of bank clerks and fellow rugby players, a young academic from Dublin, dripping with drink, confronted me. 'You're a friend of Christine Canavan's, aren't you?' I nodded. 'Well she's in a mental hospital in Limerick.'

That ancient unchristened banshee had tapped me on the shoulder once more. I froze, miles away from rudimentary merriment. A ghost smudged towards me, Christine's face looking in a window of a confectionery shop on a misty day.

I couldn't tell Laura what was wrong. She wouldn't have understood. Or at least it was important for me to expect her not to understand. On our way to Kerry on our honeymoon I stopped to see Christine. In draconian black, face washed of freckles, pale, graceless. I asked her how she was. She replied 'Well, well.' I asked her where she'd been. Paris. I didn't want to know the rest but Ireland being as it is I discovered her boyfriend had renegued on her in Paris, gone south to Greece, left her a runaway.

'I met Picasso in Paris,' she told me in Limerick mental hospital, 'I wanted to tell him about us, you and me, Liam and Sarah. There were paper carnations on the table. It was at an American woman's house. Gerry was with me. He began quoting poems by Eoghan Ruadh O Súilleabháin and I spoke eventually to myself, under the Irish of Eoghan Ruadh O Súilleabháin, I said, "Life is as a tribe of birds, some of whom hit the sun, others who fail, fail utterly." ' She was quite clear saying this, clear as though her madness was feigned but when I looked closer at her I saw her pupils had separated somehow from her eyes and were planets in space.

Kerry was Kerry. Kerry patterned by the abysmal ocean. I couldn't help thinking of her, even with Laura in a newly constructed hotel surrounded by Americans. 'Life is as a tribe of birds.'

The birds of winter were already flying low over the estuaries and planes hit their target of Shannon.

I sat on a veranda one evening, an American lady in a mink coat beside pots of geraniums nearby, troubled by scratching of planes, their lights blotted in the sky, and considered the intriguing distances between a few people once so irrevocably close.

Laura and I had three children in a very short time, christened Patrick, Annabelle and Jason. Liam's father retired, left town for County Down and I, managing my father's business now, needing more space, bought Liam's home on the forefront of the street. I was closer to a road leading nowhere in particular but to the country, closer to the leaves, had an expansive garden temporarily bleached of memory by my childhood.

But that loss of memory was destined not to last too long. Walking that garden somewhere in the early sixties, face to the sun, sun splashing the oak tree, I realized it was upon me again, life, wonderment at being alive. The voices of the orphans sounded more distant but a childhood, always buried, was now present, herbs, parsley, paprika, books with daring illustrations of Russian princesses, buckets on some plaintive sunlit Connemara beach.

To protect myself I gave wildly to my children. I journeyed to Dublin, city which was dreamily committing suicide, bought expensive books of legend for my children, books about Conne-mara kings and queens, books by Anderson and Grimm.

What was it that reminded me? The spring breeze on my shoulder as I stood outside a second-hand bookshop, a passage from Simone Weil: 'All the horrors which come about in this world are like the folds imposed upon the waves by gravity. That is why they contain an element of beauty. Sometimes a poem such as the Iliad brings this beauty to light.' I was drawn back again, conquered by young men and women on bicycles. I was in love with some imprint that had never quite dissolved, a shadow on the wall, a hieroglyphic of sun on a house like Sarah Thompson's house as it stood consumed by shadow on a late summer's day.

Irish troops were sent to the Congo on a United Nations mission, some were murdered and came embalmed in coffins. This time we mourned heroes of peace.

Rows broke out in Irish parliament over one Conor O'Brien who according to all and sundry was manhandling Katanga. The rugby team went north and played on Unionist pitches. We found the Northerners could laugh and down whiskey with us. Perhaps they weren't quite so bad after all. Old wounds were healing, a new solidarity knitting middle-class and middle-class in Ireland. Laughter in a Portadown rugby house reverberated across Ireland, the laughter of the well fed, the expensively clothed. The rugby captain in Portadown had the same twinkle in his eyes as the rugby captain in Cork.

When John F. Kennedy was assassinated a new and peculiar note struck up in Laura. She took to wearing black and walking the town, woodland trapped by mists, emulating the poetic grief of Jacqueline Kennedy. Something had been trying to rise from Laura for a long time, something perhaps as simple as change. After three children she swore to having no more, birth pangs excessive for her, the trauma of bringing forth. Mother-hood far from resigning her to an uncomplicated life opened areas in her, the nights when her children were born, their screams of pain.

Sometimes she asked me questions about the house – knowing I'd known the people who had lived there – but I was unwilling to answer. The chandelier was the same but walls were painted over and books long gone, the Newmans, the Tennysons, the Rupert Brookes and the odd rather bewitched copy of Virginia Woolf. Instead now the house was ingrained by legal books, Trojan American paperbacks.

I held my youngest child, Jason's hand as the trees were cut down, all but one or two. And even they were drastically curtailed. The men's club had long gone and even those trees, the two trunks looking ridiculous and ashamed, disappeared in time. Jason, my son, pointed to a bed of freshly fallen leaves under the truncated trees. 'Birdies,' he said, mistaking chestnuts for thrushes. We both stood, father and son, dumbfounded.

Laura began gardening and the garden produced again. The orphans wailed. Blackbirds dived to deaths. Clouds reigned, building the patterns of childhood, castles and synagogues in Russia. Laura read her first book by a serious author. William Faulkner. Things changed after that. The country girl became more sure of herself and her cheekbones stood out like toadstools. Her eyes, brown, were now glazed, her hair tied back, her gait alive and certain.

We threw a party one night when a composer of Irish music was visiting town and – in the strange way art and politics mingle in Ireland – Laura's father was there and a host of leprechaun-looking political administrators were present. The man had given a recital in town and somehow our house was chosen to entertain him afterwards, a vestige of importance descending, hen-like local councillors arriving, wine and Guinness flowing, a banquet ensuing and a fire blazing. Laura was in her element, in black, arms showing, a sherry of commitment in her fingers and the composer's children in bright jerseys railing about.

I was again aware of paintings of women of Aran. I was again aware of a chandelier shedding trinkets of shadow. I looked up, expecting a sign or a symbol from the ceiling but none was forthcoming other than the shadow of glass. Gossip dispensed with, the party hauling to a halt, the composer sat by a harpsicord provided for him and played songs, tunes that reverberated of eighteenth-century Ireland, songs about pirates and cavaliers and women who mourned runaway aristocrats by the ocean. A woman stood beside him, his wife, a tall lady with a high tragic forehead and everyone was touched, ignorant politician and local grocer by an unconquerable spirit and the nobility of an artist, his fingers tapping, his hair white and his forehead framed into a tightness and a brevity of control.

Laura held many parties after that, inviting the local drama club and ladies' society, the house again reverberating with change, crackers pulled, laughter issuing forth, the girlish laughter of women who'd never known sex. Paint peeled, old wallpaper revealed itself, ornate pinks and French boudoir blues. Something was pulling us to Moscow, a woman again walked, albeit slow at first, a sleep walker. Our house was taken over by the ghost of Elizabeth Kenneally.

It had been unpeopled when I moved in, the past gone but now shadows returned, swift as the spitting of flame. Not just the ghost of Elizabeth Kenneally haunted the house but other ghosts, ghosts of the Irish artists of the 1940s, the actor who almost took off his trousers, the soprano and the maker of stained glass. The wraiths of fog in the morning suggested the wraiths of fog in the 1940s when the caravans of travelling Shakespearian companies rested on the green and when gypsies, more colourful than they were now arrived and stayed for weeks. I could hear again Elizabeth's voice. 'It was snowing in Moscow then. The cabin rose above the cornflowers. A raft came down the river bearing peasants. My mother went mad that year. An old Bolshevik stared at me. My doll, my doll.' And I could most hear about the doll, the one she lost, the irrecoverable doll. She spoke at night when the children slept. She went over it again in detail. Her childhood, the church near their home, the Revolution, the city without lights and the beggars, her flight to the country, her mother playing the piano for lecherous gamekeepers, her mother's exasperating and bewildering disappearance into a forest of birches which merged into a forest of firs.

Snow flowers, buttercups, cornflowers, the flowers of Mrs Kenneally's childhood addled my head, most of all the poppies, a poppy of blood on a donkey's back near Ryazan, a poppy on a Bolshevik's kaftan, a scarlet scarf on his neck, a single poppy of triumph in a field of summer corn, the triumph of memory, of unmitigating love.

Laura knew what was happening and asked after her. She perceived the wallpaper peeling, saw the cracks in the ceiling, felt the floorboards going from beneath her. She walked in the garden. She untied her hair. Laura changed, a woman on a tightrope.

I walked the streets of the town by myself sometimes. It too was changing. Prosperity somewhere revealing itself. By the prom over and over again I observed a certain couple meet, a boy from middle-class background, hair brushed back poetically, a girl from lower class background and knew a certain courage to be pushing forward in the young. One condemnation of us I suppose, my college friends, one radical revelation of some falseness was that we kept to our own, the cosseted, those picked out by Mammon for a spiritual appetite. The prosperity of my meeting with those others was still with me, Sarah, Liam, Christine, Jamesy, but something of its axis was hatcheted.

It might have been the death of Camus that did it, an unheralded accident on a French motorway, or Christine's death – Christine had committed suicide in a mental hospital roughly the same time as young Irish soldiers were butchered in the Congo. Whatever, it wasn't that important; it was something more radical that had been between us, and I named that radicalism now.

It had been the ghost of Elizabeth Kenneally. She had transcended class, steam of rugby baths, wine of Dublin cafés. Her urgency, her truth had strode on through time. It had elicited a decision from the indecisive Sarah, an exile from Liam, from me now a slow reckoning with wife, time, and childhood.

The prom was marked by knifed confessions of love, initials on trees, benches. A boy sat on a red bench, reading Keats and drinking coke. A girl stood under a tree, hair tied by a ribbon, gathering some words together as she stared into the distance. I understood these young, their need for novelty, their reaching for something that only time could define for them and yet now was a reality because they believed it.

Laura began having literary parties. She gathered women of the town together, doctor's wives, solicitor's wives who would normally be playing bridge and they discussed the works of James Baldwin or Alejo Carpentier. A retrograde Jesuit dined with them and they discussed Teilhard de Chardin.

Censorship was lifting in Ireland; the books that had once been the guarded secrets of the Kenneallys were now given to the world; the artists declared to have been obscene and indecent marched in, Fitzgerald, Hemingway, and little was heard again of censorship. A country was quietly becoming cosmopolitan.

At a New Year's party Laura drank too much. She broke down, but having now read the works of most of the major modern writers her breakdown was eloquent and controlled. She spoke about this country, always divided within itself, the gombeen politicians and the quack artists.

'I want to live,' she said simply, 'I want to live.' And she walked out.

I suppose Laura's outburst is what I always associate with the first shots in the North. The first volley of death. At first not admitted or celebrated as a phase in the development of civil liberties, an ugly monster soon raised its head.

Our adversity we knew to be history.

My children grew up to the daily headlines and news broadcasts of war, a mini-war, a war of the petrol bomb and the bomb under the café counter, injuring and blowing people to pieces.

91

Patrick, Annabelle and Jason verged on adolescence, couched by affluence, not knowing things like class weren't quite so simple as they used to be. They kicked ball with the poor. They insisted on dressing in rags. I recalled Liam, his elegance at twelve, wondered if I could trade him for Patrick, decided on Patrick, little boy, in grubby jeans, dancing flirtatiously about a football.

When thirteen men were shot dead early in the year 1972, Laura, her finger cut and bleeding, snow rummaging and rifting in the garden outside, dwelt some moments on her wound, then said, 'It's funny how history repeats itself. Men never learn. We live by the wages of our own inhumanity to men. We build skyscrapers, block the earth with machines but a few simple lessons escape us, that there is no God worth talking of, no idealism worth living for except the simple precept of kindness.' Laura had ceased going to mass. She sat by an oak table, sole legacy from the Kenneally dynasty, and finished by saying. 'May God have mercy on their souls.'

I was thirty-seven now. Numbed I sat near her. Patrick entered the room, sensed something, stood.

'Mammy,' he said eventually, 'can I watch Bob Hope on television tonight?'

Laura went away that spring by herself. She bought beautiful things for herself, often second-hand coats, ancient crockery, brooches. She wore lizards and rabbits. She locked D. H. Lawrence in her cupboard and kept a clock beside her bed – we slept in separate beds now – that told her the time, that told her to wake early and concoct strange French recipes to entertain her friends with in the evening. I was left out of the picture of her mind.

Sometimes around then Liam rang.

Driving North to Derry on a May morning I concentrated on the effects of sunlight on the hills leading to Derry, dashes of rainbow and exuberances of gold, to avoid thinking.

The previous night had left an unusual aura in my mind, it had been exceptional for me to be alone, unique even to wake alone and confront the sea. It had not been unpleasant. I accepted it now as one would the tension of waiting at a railway station. I'd dressed somehow more carefully that morning, realizing that my clothes when I looked at them were not all they should have been, starched vests, navy trousers. There was a voice in the middle of my demeanour which asked for change. The formalities undergone, a British army post passed, I headed to the city centre to meet Liam. There was a vanguard march in Derry that day. Hordes were held up next to Craigavon Bridge. A lone piper played 'Amazing Grace', crowds hurled abuse from buses and two hitchhikers bearing flowers, gave sprigs to British soldiers while lunatic remnants of the Shankhill Road in Belfast shouted at them 'Go back to San Francisco, you flower children ye.'

I walked to the city centre, each step leaving an element of me behind. The hills around Derry were bequeathed with flowers, they sung with buttercups, and altogether there were no signs of war in these hills, signs of a glorious Maytime infused with sun.

He sat on the steps of Guildhall, at first no older than I'd last seen him, broader though, face ruddied and orange with sun, hair sand-coloured rather than blond, and his overall appearance governed by a multi-coloured jersey, a jersey of blue and white and yellow and green and red. He smiled, the smile of a seventeen-year-old boy. I wanted to tell him there and then to go away. He tugged me into his hand-clasp. I said, 'How are you?' In moments we were walking through the streets and he was telling me about his time away from Ireland, fifteen years which any day I could take up like rotten apples and throw in the face of the presiding spirit of this island, if there was any, and being none in the face of all those who hurt and inflict injury on those blessed by the gods with a little more sensitivity than their fellows.

I told him about myself first, a few brief sentences, then he launched into an account of himself, the first time he discussed himself he said in years.

When he first arrived in California Liam Kenneally, a student from Ireland in a long woodbine cigarette coloured coat, had been a brusque mixture of hope, despair, nonchalance. Somewhere buried deep inside him had been his mother's splintered grief, the animating colours of a stained glass window in a remote Irish church, the face of one Sarah Thompson, crushed like a yellow rose. He'd made the requisite gestures towards reorganizing his life, staying with an uncle at first, then discovering an apartment for himself in Berkeley. A student from Ireland with an ability to walk the verdure of Berkeley in a red check shirt even on the dampest of days, he commenced his studies, Ireland generating only a distant reality, a flag, limply flying, streets of Dublin fettered with nuns. He decorated his apartment with the photographs of writers, read Hart Crane by a rose light, often wondering had it been real, years of growing up, his mixed heritage, the limestone street whence he came and the trees at the end of the street, more certain with time, larger, less debased.

All the time though in his ears were Christine's words, her eyes, searching out his vulnerable spot, fixating on it with lewd grinning hatred. The girl who'd approached him so innocently once had done him harm and in doing harm intensified a portrait of Ireland, maker of wounds, tormenter of youth, ultimately breaker of all that was sensitive and enriched by sun, rain, wind.

Liam Kenneally retreated into himself, urging towards some point of self-annihilation and yet that point could not be identified as self-annihilation because it produced thoughts, long and rich, and discourses on the nature of being. Like Aphrodite Liam gained something in his loss of nation; he was bequeathed the sight of the Pacific, the slenderness of Golden Gate Bridge and a new country, one built with pain and effort, each image gained only with a maximum of precision, images of roses of Sharon buried beneath the tramline and poets, beards flourishing on them like down, reading their zany poems in pubs illumined only by the neon trickle of the juke-box.

After Christmas Liam began going out, to dances, to parties, to ice-cream parlours where cherries stood perilously above ice-cream sundaes. He met many young American girls, hair curled like rolls of butter in an Irish country kitchen, lips the optimistic red of 1958, but their friendship only prevailed as far as being invited to their parents' home for dinner. For the moment Liam lived without his body, Christine having injured deeply, destroyed the growing nature of a young man.

Early in 1958 Liam travelled south to view the first of the nomads living on Big Sur, those already blackened by sun, their children like gypsy children and their homes of redwood hidden from beach which marvelled with shadow of sky and slithers of water. It was a unique place, one which he had told me about in the second last correspondence I had from him. Something was opening in California, an unbeknownst dividend of humanity. Things were quietly spoken of, rivers in India, the *I Ching*, the *Kama Sutra* and one evening coming from Big Sur, a place far from nuns and Irish Catholic roads barren of all but the radiance of the sky, at the Santa Cruz fun-fair Liam encountered a lady studying theology in Los Angeles with whom he became friendly.

She visited him a number of times over the next few months, sleeping on his sofa, regulating his mind with passages from Martin Buber. She had red hair, wore grey suits and took a greyhound bus by the ocean to see him. Her drive was uncommon. Her father a doctor in Beverly Hills, she was of wealthy stock and carried herself, an erstwhile Bacall, a model in Paris, a lady journalist with the *Washington Post*. Her demeanour recalled all these things and more. In white blouses she commandeered Liam's attention, invoking from him tales of his garden and his mother, photographs of young Irishmen doomed to Prussian guns. In June he finished his thesis and by a mixture of events moved north with Sandra, the lady from L.A.

They found a redwood cottage near Arcata, an Indian preservation, lived there, a running stream outside their cottage and a manifold vision of redwood trees, their tops clouding the flight of birds.

They did not once make love, an area in Liam like a shelled village, like a broken sage, like a woman crying out and begging in Famine Ireland after the loss of her children. Some grievance would not let up, Christine's eyes spelling her brand of hatred.

He was guilty because she told him so and then one evening quietly he and Sandra made love, her body bigger than Sarah's, more hospitable. Ireland passed out, a most ancient grief. He lay between her breasts, a child. His mouth made for her pubic hair, waited there. Her hand went to his head, stirred a curl or two. He was without country now, without past. He was free.

We walked through the streets of Derry that afternoon until we came to a hall wherein a meeting was to be held. Liam had come to Ireland with a young girl from Derry who studied in Berkeley. This meeting was one of the many thrown up by anarchists and revolutionaries and as such women with mops about their heads stood outside the hall, waiting for news of the latest development in the world revolution while young women from diverse foreign countries teemed about in long skirts excited by this talk of revolution brewing in Derry.

I was introduced to Liam's friend, a filigree red-head who looked at me with blazingly clear eyes. Her name was Marie. California had not disturbed her Derry accent. Her skin was as the skin that advertised powder. 'Glad to meet you,' said she, 'I've heard a lot about you.'

The meeting commenced with a man of amazing courage saying that the world was changing and that the time had come to lift the sky and throw off the remnants of imperialism.

We were on the outskirts of Free Derry, a zone cordoned off by the Provisional I.R.A. and the Official I.R.A. It belonged to the people and anarchists, Trotskyites, Stalinists from European countries gloated while a certain cartoon played out, women with mops on their heads speaking of dirty diapers and burnt lamb chops. To affirm the statement of the first youth a sluggishly fat girl rose and quoted a poem by Mao Tse-Tung.

'A thousand years and more ago came Wei Were
Brandishing his whip and drove east to Kieche
As he tells in his poem.
Now the sad autumn wind is still the same
But the world has changed.'

A Protestant rector from Paris spoke in French to his brothers
and sisters of the revolution. He was the pacifist in the throng.
A baby squealed. A British soldier looked in, went out. Deter-
mined warriors sat while he reminded his audience in English
of Gandhi. Liam's girl curled in a corner, another child of war.
This time Liam was in love with a girl who'd brought him back
to Ireland to display to him her people and their plight.

Afterwards in a confusion of words we arranged to meet
Liam's friend in a house by Lough Swilly, over the border,
where both were staying. We walked on. Evening had come.
Light stood in transit. World War I was suggested, broken and
disturbed buildings. Rounding a corner we confronted a young
soldier, twenty-two, twenty-three, standing, legs apart, unaware
of us, hand perched on his rifle, singing, with a backdrop of the
buttercup hills 'Scarlet Ribbons'. We entered Free Derry, pass-
ing first a convoy of Official I.R.A., masks over their faces, then
a guard of Provisional I.R.A., all but one with masks over their
faces. The one without a mask was exceptionally beautiful, dark
haired, eyes emerald, reasoning, grinning. The reasons he did
not wear a mask he told us was because his face was already
known to the British army, he having blown up the post office
in Strabane. He laughed about his feats, promising more, yet
fear, pain in his childish remarks, a knowledge that any moment
he could expect an army bullet.

We journeyed further, climbing the Creggan. A woman de-
monstrated to us where her son of nineteen was killed on Bloody
Sunday and by a wooden cross Liam left a marigold.

Young men speeded in stolen cars, armalite guns sticking out
the windows and way up, over Derry, Our Lady of Peace stood,
her eyes shooting in a crazy fashion as though she too was victim

of a bullet. I lived on this island all my life yet I'd never been to this city – Liam in his boldness had led me there – I was impressed, moved, horrified.

Some weeks before a young Derry soldier serving in the British army had been shot dead by the I.R.A. A woman looked out on the television aerials of Derry. 'I thought the Free State army would come once like fairy horsemen. They didn't. Then the I.R.A. came. My son's in the I.R.A. I support him. But God you kill a lad of twenty-two, someone you've known since his mother was wheeling him in a pram and you wonder is any border worth the trouble. I think then I'd rather live on my social security from the Queen and send my children on a boat to London rather than to see this fighting go on and on.'

We left her. Liam was perplexed, saddened. He'd come with his girlfriend, briefed by her about the violence done to her people but now another picture emerged, that of a community, somewhere in its heart Trojan, being used, abused, led astray and yet not stumbling from the only concept they could hold on to, courage. We drove in my car out to the house on Lough Swilly, just in time for tea.

The house was occupied by students who'd organized the day's meeting, mainly these affiliated with a Christian Marxist group. Tea was a flourishing cauliflower au gratin. We feasted and afterwards spoke of Marx, God, South Africa, Biafra, Brazil, Ecuador, all those areas needy of student Marxist Christian consciousness.

A young girl from Antrim, her father a Protestant landowner, told how she supported the Provisional I.R.A. 'I was brought up on lies,' she said, 'now I want to turn those lies on my parents. With guns if need be. Guns are justified if they tell the truth. The Provisional I.R.A. is the army of the Northern Irish people.' Her frail figure curled in a corner. She stuttered her words with a special vindictiveness.

Outside one could view the ocean. Evening was coming, entrailing the bay in a deep spreading lilac.

I could see she suffered by virtue of being Protestant. She was

contrite. Faces confronted her, all these young Christian Marx-
ists from all corners, justifying in this instance the use of the
sword. Liam's girlfriend spoke of her Derry upbringing, a
cardigan on her shoulders, the squalid flats, endless deaths and
dole-queues, the timber partition between her mother's and her
father's beds as her mother died of leukaemia, the prevailing
partition between people, the ultimate boat out, a river leading
to the sea, away from the factories and the churches and the
damp portals where men discussed billiards, racing or the heart-
aches of their wives.

She'd been lucky, securing a scholarship to Berkeley, studying
now but that opportunity given her she intended to make use of
it. Her city was one fraught by the effects of imperialism. I in
my ignorance wondered at the town whence I came with the
last of the leaves at the end of the street. My country, the Irish
republic, had been less than mindful of the Northern Catholics
but then again one million Protestants lived here who would not
give up the ghost of a puppet monarch so easily. I wished I'd
done something earlier but my class had bound me, the rugby
celebrations, the allegiance to uniformity and conformity and
oddly enough I thought of Sarah, her revolution, a revolution
never realized but spluttering now, a myriad mad demagogues
let loose and a few utterly misguided men of heroism.

I walked with Liam by the ocean. His youth haunted me,
haunted his face. The Earls of Ulster had once fled from this
harbour. He told me how his woman left him in 1965 and went
to India, how he worked in a café in Berkeley when the riots
broke out. One night a naked youth from Kentucky, high on
drugs, ran into the riots, shouting about his grandmother's hens.

Then, modestly, Liam said, 'I became a tutor in Berkeley. I
met Marie a year ago. For years I was troubled by Ireland.
Marie brought me the opportunity to look more closely at a
country I left, a country divided, my shame, our shame, a
country without hope.'

I wanted to tell him that the urge I enjoyed most in life was making love to my wife. But I couldn't; that was beyond politics. I saw him by Lough Swilly, Liam Kenneally, and I knew him to have inherited his mother's alarm at the cosmic state. I repeated his name to myself. I no longer knew this man. He was coming with the political folly of a Californian college. I had my wife to look after, my children. I wanted to turn away and go home but suddenly I looked around. Liam was throwing a stone in a pool reflecting a sky of sapphire and the odd warning dash of scarlet. He hadn't changed. He was still here, some point inside him in abeyance to childhood.

Young people strummed out songs on guitars that night, the usual Northern coterie, 'Carrickfergus', 'My Lagan Love'. They were innocent as thirteen-year-olds. War, violence was forgotten. Stars came out over Lough Swilly and people in the bay slept soundly, a few lights flashing, Liam sleeping with his 23-year-old love and me wondering about my wife and my children.

Over breakfast next day Liam said he intended driving to see his father that evening. It had been fifteen years since he'd laid eyes on him. I was driving back to Galway. 'You'll come to visit us, won't you?' I said.

'Sure. Sure.' And over breakfast I saw his eyes were distant and he was looking at a boy who stood in a leather jacket before a rock pool on the strand.

Laura wanted to know all about it. The weekend, Liam, Derry. She knew Liam to have lived in this house.

'He sounds strange,' she slurred over lunch on Monday and I knew she wondered, that wonder was her domain now, that there were areas in her opening and that even on this May Monday her summer dress proclaimed a new and courageous freedom. 'His mother sounds so strange,' Laura said.

Liam rang on Wednesday. He'd seen his father, an old man living in County Down and somehow the sight had dispelled all sentimentality in him, his father grown old, compelled into an antique hat, his eyes bearing all the burning sadness of the past. Liam was returning to California, sad, uncharitable to past

100

figures. 'I've decided to return early,' he said, 'I don't think I can make it to Galway. It would take too long. I'm going back. Flying to London. Then back to California. Goodbye Sean. Maybe you could come to California some time. You and your wife.'

He put down the receiver. That was it, Liam gone. But now that Laura knew a bit, she asked more, about Liam, my exact relationship with him, his mother, and a woman who had only vaguely been on the edges of her mind for years now fermented and grew, talk of Elizabeth Kenneally was everywhere, her drowning and even my children became aware that a legendary lady once lived here, a Russian who drowned herself. The sole reality that confronted me were books on Russia, books by Russian authors, reproductions of ikons and Laura procured a photograph of Elizabeth Kenneally, admired it, showed it to our children. 'The snow queen,' Laura called her and looked at me as though accusing me of killing Elizabeth Kenneally. 'There's so much you don't know, isn't there,' she said.

I was trapped in a criminal trespass. I'd lied. I'd pretended I was ordinary whereas I'd had an extraordinary buried past.

Laura, naked in our bedroom one day, said to me, 'Liam. You were in love with him, weren't you?'

I worked. I saturated myself in the travail of local cases yet a poisonous flower flourished. My wife trembled before the tree of knowledge. She bid me tell it all, right down to the woman who made stained glass windows.

And she said, 'Remarkable the beauty of stained glass. Light coming through. Those odd windows in rural churches of doves or the Archangel Michael. The secret places in the human heart. Light coming through. A revelation.'

I told her all now, Liam, Sarah, myself. She listened. 'Sarah,' she said simply. 'You mentioned her before. She must have been lovely.' I tried to steady her but my wife was not to be calmed. She shouldered off any complicity. There was a journey that had to be done alone.

My children looked leaner, gawkier, less in the garden. They fired guns with less enthusiasm and observed their mother, burdened by pain. Laura recognized the fact, that inside me was a shattered area, an area unbound by time, a nucleus given to Liam, Sarah and the ensuing bicycles of Dublin.

In the next few years I opened a branch of my firm in Dublin. I was a big name. I dealt now in trivial and arch matters. I often journeyed to Dublin, seeing to the other branch of my business, dealing in matters of political eminence, leaving two young solicitors to look after the business at home.

Patrick was fourteen, a tall gawky boy, torn between war comics and books about the Second World War and Gandhi. Annabelle never left a picture of David Bowie, and Jason, true to his name, searched every crevice in the garden for wrens' nests and thrushes' nests.

My office in Dublin overlooked a street of trees. I was back in a city I'd sworn to forfeit for ever. I had the same view that I had nearly twenty years before. Occasionally a beautiful girl would pass outside and all manner of misfortune was forgone. I remembered Sarah, Sarah walking by blindly in white, and this discovery of memory was not bitter. It was sweet even, tranquil and unabased as lace hankies long ago.

On a Friday in May 1974, having left my office, returning to my car parked in the centre of the city I witnessed the effects of one of a triad of bombs that went off about 5.30, rush-hour. I was rounding a corner when the bombs exploded. I tried to help. There was little one could do. Newspaper vendors threw the evening paper over bodies smashed in blood. Children miraculously still wandered. Cars were blown to gnarled turnips. Blood ran and odd bits of garment and clothes identified themselves. An old man whispered the Act of Contrition to someone's ear and I noticed a child's school-book, its pages ripped out but one remaining, that of a tree with a little girl in a Red Riding Hood costume. Ambulances screamed about. Old women spoke rosaries. I was not a doctor or a priest and I soon vacated the place, driving back towards Galway.

I had been away two weeks. Laura was frantic with worry.

102

Light had not left the sky and the tree out in the garden, over the wall which cut garden from yard, stood out against the sky.

The children were still out, Patrick gone to a hop in aid of the swimming-pool. Annabelle was visiting the house of a new friend, a girl with whom she shared intimate secrets. Jason was riding a blue bicycle by the river.

Later that evening, cutting carrots, Laura quietly told me she was having an affair. 'I'm in love,' she said. She'd been seeing the boy, a young photographer, for six weeks now. They'd been sleeping with one another for four. He took photographs of local weddings, of young girls with candy coloured smiles at their first Holy Communion. His photographs were exhibited in a window outside his studio. But also there were sometimes photographs of rural scenes, picturesque faces. He had an eye for oddity, the crooked smile, the collapsing cottage. He was from the area, was young, talented, one of the first of the young to return to the town after going away to study.

I sat down. I had been away a lot, true, I myself had sometimes slept with other women, young girls in a small rural hotel after a rugby outing. I would never have expected Laura to sleep with anyone though, read James Baldwin, yes, flirt with his negro angst, entertain Jesuits, have semi-lesbian relationships with literary minded, bridge-playing bankers' wives, but an affair, my wife, it shattered me. Laura, the country cinema-going maiden, turned mature woman, breasts, eyes, pubic hair consumed by a youth who did not even play rugby. I buried fingers in my fists, a child holding a clump of daisies. 'All right,' I said, 'It's your choice. I cannot tell you what to do.'

'It's an affair,' Laura said, 'It will end.'

'All right.'

'Sean,' she smiled.

'Yes.'

'There's something about Elizabeth Kenneally I don't know. Did she sleep with the man people said she was in love with or is it all rumour?'

'She slept with him.'

103

'How do you know?'

I looked at her, shocked at her question. I didn't know before now except in the sense I'd been between her legs. I too had been in love with Elizabeth Kenneally. The whole world had been in love with her and slept with her and left her so all she could do was drown herself.

Patrick came in first; Annabelle returned at one and Jason cycled the avenues of town until two in the morning, a child gone mad.

With the same fatalism as Liam Kenneally put Billie Holiday records on our gramophone in Dublin a long time before I knew my marriage was running into irascible difficulties. There were the children, there was the town; its henna coloured spaniels, its old women. There were my expanding offices in Dublin. My name spoke of integrity in Irish legal circles but when I got the offer of a job with an international prisoner's rights organization I left work placing young men of accomplishment in my offices.

I left Ireland in November 1975. I went to live in London. My marriage had speeded to a halt. Laura was none the worse for it, wearing regimental blacks, decorous jewellery, a limited quantity of make-up. She had begun doing something she had never done before, illustrating Irish folk stories, collecting tales, illustrating them with the refined colours of her imagination and with a delicate pen, spending laborious hours in the sitting-room, bowed over pen and light drawing-paper. Sometimes she came to stay with me, she and the children. Sometimes they came alone, most often Patrick.

London at first was the changing of the guards for them or some fat lady like the fish lady at home outside a sex shop, but gradually they saw it, a major city, visits to it changing them, my children, from Irish waifs disturbed by American T.V. programmes to young intelligent erudites, open to much, appreciative of a lot, indicating things to me which I myself would not have seen. Ireland blurred out. It would have gone altogether were it not for bombs and my work. I studied photographs which indicated bruises deep as clouds over the Comeragh mountains on prisoners convicted of bombings. I spoke to these men, men from Antrim or Belfast, rarely from the republic; they'd been brought up on a diet of Pearse and flags and tales of heroism. They'd been nurtured by church and state to violence, church by its opposition to Northern government, state by its evil annihilation of life from Catholic workers in the North. I distrusted these men yet was overcome somehow by pity. These men, one or two from the South, could have been me had I the anger or the ignorance. I had not the anger but ignorance is something I suppose people choose, not to see all the possibilities, that there are other ways. Myself, I could not sacrifice my children to bombs. Besides I would not vaunt Protestant opinion in Northern Ireland but feeling desperate enough perhaps I should burn myself alive in Donegall Square in Belfast relating to people not the profound injustice done to the Catholic population but an incomprehensible situation, one born of ignorance and oppression, stalemated into two groups who would never understand one another except by force of some miraculous personality.

Still I talked to prisoners, those convicted of doing incalculable damage to human life. I unerringly took down their statements. I wanted to tell the world that once punished by law you couldn't go on punishing people for ever for crimes, no matter how terrible, done in an insane state, yet somehow telling of other people's inability to act, other people's inability to comprehend the obdurate suffering of minorities.

A man from Antrim told me he left a wife at home with two children. 'Here I am abused, bullied, shit, piss thrown on me. But there is one thing I recall,' he said, 'even when they're looking at me as though I am a bull with foot and mouth disease, I remember the first time I met my wife. In a café in Ballymena and Roy Orbison was singing "Silence is golden".'

I was a different kind of Irish person in England, one educated, representing a republic born in the conflagration of civil war. I came looking over the other side of the fence, at those not so fortunate.

I endured in a flat in Kensington but I could also see each time a bomb went off how it was the women in the canteen or the men on the road who suffered. I knew that violence was no way to peace. It hurt those who performed it, it hurt those not directly connected with it, the ordinary Irish in England, those leading humdrum lives. It explained nothing. It injured the ancient spirit of Ireland, the one Laura delineated in her line-drawings with their splashes of colour, a swan over a lake, a king on a white horse, a monk lighting the Christian flame on a hill-top.

I was quite scientific about my work. I spoke to Laura about compromises, she coming to live in London or perhaps all of us living in Dublin, but something bound her to a simple town in the western midlands, leaves perhaps bordering it or the nuns nearby, tending honey-combs, educating children in Gaelic songs or merely drawing in coloured chalks ikons on the black-board of woods and trees and little girls bearing baskets of primroses in typical nun mentality of untainted childhood and unshedding trees.

I was sitting in a café late one evening, work of an evening done, the British Library shut, when I saw a woman sitting by a table near the window who at first moved me and stilled me with remembrance. She was about forty, blonde, eyes dark with the dark of an amethyst, lips slightly painted, yet for all of middle-age with a peculiar bird-like quality, that of an anxious sparrow. She was addressing herself to an older smaller woman. I listened. They spoke of school. Problems they were encounter-ing. Rows with men in authority. Changes in the system. I waited for the thing which would identify her and then I heard it, a trace, an Irish accent.

Sarah. I went over to her. She saw who it was immediately, not surprised, having the manner of one who ushered in every-thing with an air of inevitability.

'It couldn't be.'

In minutes she was taking out a brand of French cigarettes, having introduced me to her friend, a fellow teacher. Sarah was headmistress of a girls' comprehensive school.

I talked to her until the café shut. She did not want to go to a pub but invited me to her home, an apartment not far from mine. She told me she was truly astonished to find me working and living in London, that it all seemed so far away and long ago, Ireland, that she was thinking of returning there. Her mother ran a clinic. Unwed she was thinking of going back there and living with her mother for a while.

These encounters took place early in the spring. They were as unreal as glass marionettes. I journeyed delicately to her apartment, all the spring breezes of London ushered in. We talked of long ago, of now, of her endless problems with the girls, of their lives bound in like a concentration camp with sores, abortions, misfit boy-friends, ill-behaving parents. She was a kind of glamorous parent for them, a popular teacher, well known in London educational circles.

Sarah Thompson had left her order fifteen years before. Going to Africa she found the heat gruelling, the nuns far from being servants of Christ but slaves to Mammon, brutalizing and burning young Africans with a diseased and burdensome religion. She witnessed and tremored under the white heat of the sun; she wore blank white, she became blank white inside, only the charred crucifixes telling her of another world, another life, one of risk. She recalled her father in his weeks before dying, his face anxious as the chords of a piano, his eyes always on the same note, some point not undergone, some shame not remitted.

She heard again the clanking to Arbour Hill, saw the green on the tricolour as the green of shamrock, saw her father laying wreaths over the dead soldiers' graves. She recalled this remorseless childhood scene and wished somehow to redress it, the blackening skies. She remembered Liam, her first succumbance to sensuality, its ardour, its pain. She recalled the woman she felt in him and how she recoiled from her, Elizabeth Kenneally, a demon in a summer dress.

She recalled the nights of Dublin, the neon lights like coloured daisies and the odd Italian cafés, splashing their lights into the wet night. She recalled the plane to Africa and would have gone mad with this remembrance, the decaying hippopotamus of a plane, grounding at last, unleashing her on a continent filling and spluttering already with Irish nuns.

When the revolution came she heard the gun-shots and interpreted them. She saw pregnant women shot down, planes flying over refugees on the roads, suppressed by their baggage and the odd majestic snake still in the bushes. She wanted to cry out, ask this archetypal God whom she'd come to serve for help but realized in the deepest most crystalline part of her young Irish heart that no such God existed, that Sarah Thompson was alone, seduced by another illusion, an illusion that one must sacrifice to be.

She left.

She journeyed to England, calling on a country where bananas were piled into boats like a thousand eyes and she arrived in England, wearing woolly white cardigans sent by her mother, started teaching, having a few affairs, almost marrying, for once losing her lover to another woman, a Swede like the man. She joined many societies, sat on many boards, made many decisions but somewhere in her modern independent heart a gall-less flag still flew, the Irish tricolour, refusing warmth or solicitude, battering itself against an unjust breeze.

The woman I encountered was made of many things, different from the one I knew before, as though the past had disbanded in her and she'd started again, picking and choosing who or what she was to be. But one remnant of the past was unmistakable, a touch, a decisiveness of Liam Kenneally. You refuse entry to your past but something is still there, the unquenchable spirit of a vision, the look on the face of an eighteen-year-old boy or girl who discerns life for what it is, a flight of the spirit against a savage sun.

Sarah Tompson left London for Ireland early in the summer. She did not write to me. Our encounters folded, another page.

This time however the effects lingered and in a tropical summer in London something gave in me, I cried, sweated, I called out like one left without form in a bombing. Laura came to see me, talked to me. Even she with her foundation of rural ease did little to help. We talked of the past and eventually she, almost in the fashion of a female doctor, got to the core, some weeks in Dublin once, an affair, a triangular relationship, one buried, unspoken but always there, a mystery, a voice in itself telling of some extraordinary dance, some exciting welcome into a world of love.

'You were too affected by Liam Kenneally and Sarah Thompson,' Laura said.

'They're different from you. More meteorites than people. Jesus, Sean can't you see. They messed up your beautiful normality.'

Laura came a few times that summer. I began working again. A chance arose to go to the United States, to investigate the records of a Californian prison.

'People speak of you in Ireland,' Laura said, 'wonder why you left. Maybe if you go to California now you'll find out.'

I didn't want to go. I didn't want to see Liam again. It was all too grotesque and painful and yet I knew that Laura was right, that something was undone, some mischievous element in experience, always battering and tormenting and wending its way in. 'Sean,' she said simply, 'you've fooled yourself for years. Fooled yourself in marrying, in having children, in playing rugby. There's something in you, a disturbance, a storm-cloud never burst or maybe even gentle rain unfallen.' And she ended – it was in my apartment in London – 'I love you Sean.'

I met her in Dublin before I left. It was October. We walked through the streets. Sun was shining, leaves dallying, a saffron blaze. And we stopped to watch a street theatre show in Stephen's Green. The show was performed by exquisitely good-looking young people and told of a girl gone from Famine Ireland, given the gift of youth by Mother Ireland, who journeys through passages in American history. We encountered her at a stage in which she waltzed with the ghost of a Confederate soldier. He recited a poem to her before waltzing and my erudite ear recognized the verse, Walt Whitman.

"All over bouquets of roses,
O death I cover you over with roses and early lilies,
But mostly and now the lilacs that bloom the first,
Copious I break, I break the sprigs from the bushes,
With loaded arms I come, pouring for you,
For you and the coffins of all of you O death.'

Ireland was changing, even in the abstract and most remote part of its youth. I looked at Laura. We left the youth dressed in Confederate costume, the girl in Victorian lace and walked on, past streams of honey-coloured leaves.

In San Francisco I met many people concerned with jails. I curiously fulfilled every detail of my work. Then I went to see Liam. It was already November, winter in abeyance, the days light and blue. I'd put it off as long as possible. I was staying in San Raphael and one evening I crossed Golden Gate Bridge, the bridge zooming on top of me, to see Liam. I presumed he'd be at the address from which he last wrote me: 2248 Clay Street. Living there with Marie.

I knocked on the bottom door.

Marie answered. She looked considerably changed, dressed impeccably – in colours that would have done a rare and luxurious chocolate box proud. Her eyes were enveloped by a kind of soaked blue. She had on dark stockings, a blue dress. Her eyes were different too, no longer hard and guilty but soft, sweetened and touched by life. She bid me enter a regulated apartment. There was no question of her not recognizing me. It was all part of a drama now or a modern movie, each movement touched by ultimate psychological significance. She put on coffee. The place was warm and Californian paintings were redolent on the wall, sending off waves of good feeling.

'Funny, you should catch me here,' she said, 'I'm leaving

next week.' I did not ask about Liam. All I knew was that he wasn't there, that his presence was long gone, unfelt now, a pressure vacated for want of fulfilment. Marie asked about home, with little urgency. The dangerous revolutionary had become mistress to a San Francisco night-club owner. She'd lost her Derry accent, was now possessed of a fledgling Californian one. But she was not at all apologetic; hardened to the fact she'd changed and glowing under it even. He'd gone under such strange circumstances one could only account for it by some kind of crusade of madness, taking his things one evening, driving north to a monastery they'd once viewed together from the outside, leaving behind his clothes in a bundle in a rural hotel and joining an order of medieval Roman Catholic monks, their gowns white as wheaten bread. She'd gone to collect his clothes, antique check shirts, having a Bloody Mary in a country hotel built in New England fashion, driving off again.

'Since he left Ireland he was not to be calmed,' Marie stated. 'Fraught, fidgety, talking in his sleep. Talking as though asleep. Speaking of violence, a violence done to human beings, talking of war, grief, yes, he spoke of grief a lot, spoke about it as though it were a parent. I loved that guy, loved him with an animal desire. He's gone now, gone from you, me, all of us.'

Her last words were like a child's conclusive mantra, something she'd ordered for herself over and over again.

Liam gone, yes, Liam gone north.

'Can I see him?' I asked.

'Not unless you go back to Europe. He's in the mother house of his order now. In southern Switzerland. They are a small order founded during some imperial war in the Middle Ages to ask for peace.'

I spent a lot of time after that with Marie. I went to the night-club owned by her lover. It was fraught with the attractive people of planet Earth, women who looked like expensive parrots and men always searching the eyes of men.

Marie was moving in with her lover, leaving thoughts of Derry and confusion and vengeance. Her hair was controlled by a fine comb and she always observed things like one who had touched some grievous worry, something that continually preyed upon her brain. 'I've lost my past,' she said at last one evening, 'lost my war, lost any amendment that can be made for it.'

At Christmas I stopped in Ireland. I'd discovered virtually nothing, yet my odyssey had brought its own rewards. Fire blazed. Laura cooked triumphantly. Patrick, aged sixteen, helped her, his own version of Adonis. Annabelle played David Bowie and Mozart and Jason looked through the window, a mystic whose eyes penetrated stained glass.

I went back to London but I knew now that my years of exile were drawing to a halt, that I was going to return, reassume public responsibility. I knew too I had a journey to complete, that I was going to see Liam. His eyes, his hair came back now, all he had that I hadn't, natural gaiety, mysticism, a driving impetus towards the most truthful point. I wanted to tell him I'd envied him and perhaps killed his relationship with Sarah. I wanted to tell him that I understood if no one else did, why a young man's eyes should be fixated with a point of pain. I wanted to tell him simple things too, like how beautiful Laura looked and how full of life my children were. But something haunted, the tree in the back garden, a monument to the life of the Kenneallys, the loveliest family in town, father a brilliant doctor, mother from the abyss of the Russian Revolution, son warmed by the golden light of his mother and the pervasive intellect of his father.

In London I remembered simple things, like Liam naked, bathing, dipping with the self-consciousness of a statue over a dock leaf. I knew now that Sarah had deserted us both with all the cruelty of woman-kind, that it was no use impeaching her. She'd played her role. It could not have been otherwise.

It was January and cold. Rain fell and red buses rushed about with a sense of urgency. Many art exhibitions were held and the public were seduced by Blake and Turner. One week-end I flew to Lugano. There it was already spring and mountains enfolded would-be blossoms. I drove to the monastery Marie had told me of.

I knew now it wasn't Sarah's fault or mine but guilt had come from the past, unrelated to Sarah or me. It was willed upon Liam by his mother. She'd been a woman climbing out of a pain, who failed to make the light. Always in her eyes she ensnared a journey from her past, from all known and loved, from father and mother, photographs, brothers, a doll with smitten lips. Once you leave security you can't return. Neither can you name the abyss you travel into unless you are possessed of genius or humility. What Liam was adopting now was a stance of humility whereby he could call the darkness he'd inherited from his mother a name.

I arrived at the monastery. It was situated on a mountain-side, overlooking a village and in turn a lake. I was so possessed by her I expected Elizabeth Kenneally to answer the door but a monk not unlike Friar Tuck, fat and bald, opened the door and led me into a yard where last year's nasturtiums still existed and then into a waiting-room where I was left until the head monk arrived. He spoke in French.

'Vous cherchez Frère Antoine. Il est parti. Il a fondé une succursale de notre ordre sur une petite île en Irlande du Nord. Avec des autres il prie pour la paix.'

He had gone. With some others he'd founded a branch of the order in Northern Ireland, on a little island situated in a lake surrounded, I later found out, by the densest area of tribulation in Ireland. North or South. With the others, true to the patience and availability of the group, he asked God for peace. It was as though something had got him before me, madness, that odd visitor, fate or decision, call it what you like. Had Liam become a total clown, dressing in white, covering the earth in nasturtiums, red and gold, praying in silence? The answer I would not know until I saw him.

I packed up in London. I was going back to Ireland. I intended to live again with my wife and children, to focus on my career again, some two years of research and investigation

113

achieved in London. My children welcomed me as though I'd never gone. They addressed Laura by her Christian name now. Her eyes were very tender when she first met me at Dublin airport. 'You've changed so much,' she said, 'arches, lines, gone from your forehead.'

I returned with her to Galway but something agitated me throughout the spring and early one morning I took off, driving North. The morning was fresh and gay with spring; each time I stopped I smelt peat, the aftermath of tinkers' fires and the ridiculous scent of burnt gorse. Bogs smouldered, black. I was scared. I inveigled garages, coffee shops, anything for distraction and curiosity. Old women dwelt on coffees in Monaghan town. The border I was crossing was now a different kind of frontier. Liam told me too much about myself. I recalled the fair-haired undisciplined man I encountered in Derry some years before, the multi-coloured jersey, the eyes, smashed blue. Those eyes had perilously haunted me, drawing me back. I was settling into marriage, children again. There were a few qualms. I resisted those qualms. I knew it was over, trucking ghosts around the globe, but one thing I had to know, had Liam's eyes changed, had their pain become less definite?

British soldiers abused me. I abused them back. I was not in the mood for these divisions. Little men from Liverpool or Birmingham stood back; rarely they met anyone who reacted to their bullying. They eyed me, eyes that were sonorous, wondering, taken aback. I drove on. A mist lifted. Even in Ulster hills were emerald.

My nervousness, my preoccupation with nervousness increased, a clean-shaven table, paprika, parsley, the serious items of childhood, they were before me. I could feel the ridges on Liam's face, they were already encountering me.

As in song a boat brought me there; the natives knew of these foolish men in white, half-monks, half-harlequins. A boat-man waited. I went to an old cow-shed already being converted. A hazel tree stood outside. Big dwarf windows looked at me. A monk answered, he looked no more than fifteen. Rain stood on the distant water, a column, a rainbow jumped like a fish. I asked for Brother Anthony.

Let me tell you about this place, soft hills, manifold hills, creamy skies, troubled water, a flash, a thunder of rain. Surrounding all this tranquillity a countryside of butchery, of levelled humanity, of farmyard murder, cottage door shootings, outrage piled upon outrage. Here monks from a remote medieval order, young turned in from colleges, old men from the pursuit of learning, took the first steps towards building a base. They dressed in white, were not so much Roman Catholic as medieval Catholic; an order of the Middle Ages whose symbols were haunted by a reverence for a Godhead of peace.

I was led along a passage into a room. Young men had blue eyes that stood out like Mediterranean plants.

Liam encountered me in a rough room, smelling of newly hewn wood. I perceived a gilt-edged book somewhere behind him, a clock. His eyes looked out, the blue of a Greek sky, the blue that defied gods and blood and time and war, Liam's eyes, his mother's eyes, eyes that knew only an endless traipsing after uncertain truths and wilful lovers, eyes that somehow seemed to unite two people now, Liam and Liam's mother. I wanted to run back to the safe things, the ordinary things but quietness held me here, Liam sitting, engaging in an account of the place.

'We grow flowers, plant roses, hope somewhere that a vibration of our existence will reach this land, change something. Waging war, inner as well as outer is like banging one's head against the wall of a cell. We have come here following an ancient mandate to convince ourselves, the earth, that peace will come, that it is worth silencing ourselves for, worth waiting for.'

The simple things collapsed, the things about which I built my life, Laura, the children. I wanted to hide like a baby thrush. I coveted some posture of withdrawal now but there was no means I could shake him off; looking at Liam was like looking at the garden, at Elizabeth, at the rabbits, the mice, the tree.

115

You saw yourself. That was it. That was what brought me here. I saw myself as I had been once, shouldering innocence, weighing each choice, watchful, discerning importance in everything. Having children, feeding them, clothing them wasn't enough. There was more, some continual pageant demanded of one, sacrifice, alacrity, knowingness.

If I could I'd have gossiped, told Liam about Sarah, living again in Ireland, but he went on, the sun shining in now. 'For years I ran. I didn't know what I was running from. I searched, switched on areas of myself. There were people, colours, ideologies; I wanted to create, shape, if only a mask to hide myself from myself. Coming here is an attempt to live without betrayal. We betrayed, Sean, us, our people, we betrayed ourselves, we were the privileged few, privileged even with love. We gazed at the universe from a rampart, saw the other faces, didn't pity them. They were part of a Greek drama.'

I recalled faces, young soldiers imprisoned in photographs, their iron stares, their knowledge of death.

'And the leaves,' Liam said, 'the leaves on grey, all that was embodied in those leaves, an inner plentifulness, I have come upon again. Within myself. I'll tend to hives. Grow flowers. Shape again. With my hands. A sculpture. A recognition, a divining of that area where one registers peace, from which peace flows, a temperature, to instil itself and linger in the areas in most need of patience, those of anguish, death, death by blood, death by the killing and maiming of the spirit.'

I still wasn't convinced. Was this another of Liam's archetypal poses? He'd doffed a multi-coloured jersey for a cassock, white as early morning bread.

At least though my eyes permitted themselves to look at Liam, not as he had been but as he was now, one who had temporarily found peace, one who prayed to a God disowned by most, one who believed in life over death, in the armament of the sun over the wedges of dark in the human spirit. For that revelation, albeit only momentary, I would be grateful to him for ever.

We went outside. He introduced me to others, those with

American accents, those with European accents. He showed me a rose bush that would flower in summer, a 'revelation', he said, and suddenly, just suddenly against the lake there was something in Liam's face, a stillness like stone, one of those faces on ancient stone in Ireland weathered by rain, lightning, by decay in the face of Cromwellian slaughter and penal persecution. But whereas those faces, monastic faces on ancient crosses, were hammered in by the elements, Liam's was smashed by a different kind of weather, the weather of the spirit in pursuit of something, a clause, a cataract of mystery that would not diffuse, or perhaps merely the weather of the soul which assailed a young man in a white sleeveless jersey, rimmed by a sky-blue stripe, who cycled animatedly on an ancient faltering bicycle through the streets of Dublin, splashing through pools, looking decidedly for hot cross buns in Bewley's on a wet and windy day.

We said goodbye. Rain was falling.

Crossing by boat I wondered had it all been an illusion, this meeting on an island, peopled by poets and academics in monks' gowns?

My journey tapered South.

I could still see him, his face, his eyes, inveigled by rain against hills that had known the enslavement and death of birds and men but other things came now, Elizabeth's face, her eyes when a fire blazed in her home and a soprano sang gifted songs about bogs and early morning larks and Irish trains always askew. Christine's eyes, always pained, always fearful of catastrophe. Jamesy's eyes, our college friend, the roses in his lapel, the roses always moulting from a smart college blazer. Sarah's eyes, her masquerade, her dance, and I saw them dancing again, Liam and Sarah in a Dublin hotel, perceived and watched over by Elizabeth, the ghost who'd always harkened to music, melancholy or urgent.

Before I left Liam had told me, 'One thing haunted me all these years, not just faces of First World War soldiers in a dark County Galway men's club or the stares of young school-going boys in posh Irish schools but something else, a lady, the artist who made the glass.

'She has the ultimate triumph, her words, her recognition that light can come through stained glass. I recall one window she made, depicting the story of the Children of Lir, swans rising from human bodies.

'I stood in front of it once in a dark Irish church, with my mother, conscious of how the damp of the church affected her, conscious of her unease in this atmosphere but still aware of the beauty of the window, light smashing through blues and greens, standing out, a renaissance.

'And those swans will always represent to me the grief of Ireland, the human spirit freeing itself from human form, the pain of a nation distilling itself into tenderness. That's why I came here, to wait, watch for that moment, augment its coming because we conspired towards the pain, you and I, the faceless privileged, those with all, those ignorant of all but beauty. Now I can turn that beauty, the beauty of my mother's fireside parties into a different kind of beauty, that of reverence, the knowledge that shackles once contested can be shaken off.'

I drove through towns, limp and grey. As it was evening neon lights dashed on. Pubs opened. People rushed into them. Country and Western music urged me on my way, a bar here, a note there, the beating heart of thrifty commercial Ireland. Bog stretched, sky implored, a countryside somehow seemed less vulnerable and passing a church somewhere I stopped, parked my car, walked inside.

It was dark and tomb-like, unnourished by any work of art. I didn't pray. I desisted from prayer, just stood a moment, realizing it was over now, my search, and I could give in to the things of life, leaving Liam and his mother behind for ever. But before I left the church I thought of her, my wife, Laura, motioned to her image with the thoughts in my mind, to her hair, nose, eyes, wanting again to hold her, to tell her it was over, this running about. I walked to the porch. Rain had come, sliming through the sky.

118

I waited before entering the car, already whole patches closing in me, areas which registered the colours of a girl's scarf or the patterns on a boy's tie, areas which dwelt and lingered on sun and speed, walking then to my car, saying goodbye to Liam and Sarah, lighting a cigarette before starting the car, including Jamesy and Christine and all the Jamesys and Christines, all the vulnerable children of the fifties or whatever age they were begotten, into my farewell, starting home, her face somehow disappearing too, that already jaded ghost Elizabeth Kenneally, and a new face greeting me, that of my wife, when I arrived home, a woman of the country, hazel hair on her shoulders and a laughter in her eyes, coaxed part from peace, part from understanding.

Dublin, 28 April 1977 – Sevilla, 27 April 1979.

Germaine Greer
The Obstacle Race £5.95

the fortunes of women painters and their work

In her first book since the pioneering and bestselling *The Female Eunuch*, Germaine Greer considers the fascinating question of why there have been so few women painters of the first rank. Ms Greer demonstrates brilliantly that the answer is not hard to find: 'you cannot make great artists out of egos that have been damaged, with wills that are defective, with libidos that have been driven out of reach and energy diverted into certain neurotic channels'.

'Instils respect, asks bold questions, does not make wildly exaggerated claims' MARGARET DRABBLE, LISTENER

'Passionate yet lucid . . . a book that explains . . . the psychological, economic and even aesthetic reasons for the virtually unchallenged patriarchalism of all our artistic establishments' ERICA JONG

Herbert R. Lottman
Albert Camus £3.95

a biography

Since the tragic death in a car-crash in 1960 of Albert Camus, author, philosopher of the Absurd and comrade of Jean-Paul Sartre, the legends surrounding his brief but remarkable life have obscured the facts. Here is the first full-scale biography of Camus; a portrait not only of the man, but of the times that made him.

'A portrait of the artist, the outsider, the humanist and sceptic, simultaneously sensuous and austere, righteous and guilty, that breaks the heart' JOHN LEONARD, NEW YORK TIMES

'Herbert Lottman's life is the first to be written, either in French or in English, and it is exhaustive, a labour of love and of wonderful industry' JOHN STURROCK, NEW YORK TIMES BOOK REVIEW